Praise for *FitCEO*

"Take it from one of the top women CEOs of our time. Together with co-author Lillian So, Rebecca Macieira-Kaufmann delivers a profoundly useful guide to addressing the challenge of living a healthy life while juggling the intense demands of work. This book synthesizes the constant noise of lifestyle advice into simple, actionable tips that will change your life."

JILL KINNEY, Chairwoman, Active Wellness and Buck Institute for Research on Aging

"Rebecca Macieira-Kaufmann and Lillian So offer a thoughtful, wise approach to successful leadership that goes beyond physical, mental, emotional, and spiritual fitness. Through their concept of "habitual discipline," the remarkable commitment to one's holistic health, executives can yield extraordinary gains. CEOs would do well to adopt the creative ideas of fitness and leadership they have developed. I plan to use this approach with the executive team a' our company."

TONY ROSSABI,

"This is a delightful book and a great read for anyone looking to get more out of life. Rebecca and Lillian have written a joyful, flowing, and easy-to-read book full of great wisdom with many tips, ideas, and inspiration drawn from their own experiences. I highly recommend it!"

ALISON DAVIS, Co-founder and managing partner, Fifth Era & Blockchain Coinventors

"Macieira-Kaufmann and So have written a deceptively simple book with readily implementable practices that can transform your life. I incorporated them into my daily routine, and they made a noticeable difference immediately."

DESA SEALY, President and CEO, Gotham Urban Ventures

"As the female CEO of a publicly traded company it can be so hard to find a person, let alone a book, to give truly valuable and relevant perspective to help make my day-to-day more manageable, balanced, and fulfilling. I found myself making many notes as I read through the pages of this book of small adjustments that can make a big impact, which for me is immeasurably valuable."

JAIME LEVERTON, CEO, Hut 8 Mining Corporation

"With numerous genuine, personal examples, Rebecca and Lillian provide amazing tips and advice on adopting simple, easy practices and habits to gain sustainable mental and physical well-being. *FitCEO* is a very accessible book, cleverly playing with counterintuitive concepts such as 'Less Is More' and 'Slow Down to Speed Up.' It is a useful journey for experienced CEOs who still want to 'dream a new dream,' but also for young start-up CEOs who want to get it right from the start."

OLIVIER NJAMFA, CEO, Enghouse Interactive France

"Leaders must be fit—not just physically but also emotionally, mentally, and spiritually—to lead well in their organizations and their lives. *FitCEO* offers powerful advice and fun, doable tips, spiked with anecdotes from decades of executive leadership and an enduring friendship between the co-authors. If you find yourself in need of a tune-up (and who isn't!) get this book for yourself—and one for an accountability buddy to play along with you!"

CHARLENE LI, Founder, Altimeter; author, *The Disruption Mindset*

"*FitCEO* is an important and timely book. Integrating the various aspects of our lives and figuring out how to thrive both personally and professionally has never been easy. These days, it seems more challenging than ever. Rebecca and Lillian give us a road map that is both wise and practical, to help us be the holistic leaders of our own lives."

MIKE ROBBINS, Author, *We Are All In This Together*

"Resilient CEOs build resilient teams and organizations, but our calendars and competing agendas work against us when it comes to committing to our own physical and mental fitness. The beauty of Macieira-Kaufmann and So's book, for any senior executive, lies in its simplicity, real-world experiences, and the practical lists that make CEO fitness an achievable habit."

DAVID REIMER, CEO, The ExCo Group

"*FitCEO* is an important milestone in helping educate leaders on the importance of self-care. Macieira-Kaufmann and So skillfully articulate an easy-to-follow structure for whole-body fitness, making the book a must-read for any executive looking to increase their energy and improve their health."

DAMON SCHECHTER, Managing partner, Olam Capital; former CEO, Shipwire

"*FitCEO* is a must-read for anyone who is interested in practical and holistic advice about how to lead more effectively. The tips and tools are easy to digest and implement—even transformative. Bravo to Rebecca and Lillian for writing a gem of a book that can help even the most experienced CEOs develop their leadership muscle."

ANNE BAKAR, President and CEO,
Telecare Corporation

"*FitCEO* is a simple yet powerful guide to implementing small changes in your lifestyle to significantly impact your overall health and energy. Rebecca and Lillian provide real-world examples of incorporating sustainable practices to mentally, physically, and energetically maintain fitness. Their holistic approach is a fresh new way for any executive to view health and wellness."

MIKE HOLT, CEO, IO Integration

"Rebecca and Lillian's 'less is more' philosophy makes this an easy and rewarding read for the busiest executive. The book will serve as coach and personal trainer, outlining simple 'we can do this' steps for those who strive to be more fit leaders and human beings. Step one: read this book."

MARY HUSS, President and publisher
at *San Francisco Business Times*

"Coming up on twenty years as a CEO in California, I very much appreciate the guidance provided by Rebecca and Lillian in *FitCEO*. Using the foundation of making a Commitment, setting Boundaries, executing with Intention, remembering to balance with Self-Care, and never, ever forgetting that Heart & Soul is ultimately a major key to success, *FitCEO* will assist you in finding a life–work balance. Enjoy reading this book—it's filled with many important life lessons."

MATTHEW STEVENS, President and CEO,
The Bay Club Company

FitCEO

BE THE LEADER
OF YOUR LIFE

Rebecca Macieira-Kaufmann
and Lillian So

FIT

Achieve holistic health in your busy life—at work, home, and play

CEO

PAGE TWO

This book is not intended as a substitute for the medical advice of
physicians. Readers should regularly consult a physician in matters
relating to their health and particularly with respect to any symptoms
that may require diagnosis or medical attention.

Cataloguing in publication information is
available from Library and Archives Canada.
ISBN 978-1-77458-142-1 (paperback)
ISBN 978-1-77458-143-8 (ebook)

Page Two
pagetwo.com

Edited by Kendra Ward
Copyedited by Christine Lyseng Savage
Cover and interior design by Taysia Louie

fitceobook.com
rmkgroupllc.com
meetlillianso.com

From Rebecca: *To my home team: Gonçalo, Isaac, and Matilde—with love. To my mother and sister and all my family, friends, colleagues, and clients, who have inspired me and taught me so much on this journey: my heart is filled with appreciation and gratitude for you. And to Lillian: what fun this has been to do together!*

From Lillian: *To my parents, teachers, and mentors, for helping me learn and unlearn all the things that shape my present and future self. Thank you for all the love, energy, and guidance you have given me in order for me to become the leader of my life. Infinite gratitude to all my clients and students—past, present, and future. You are my inspiration, my muses, and the reason why I do the work I do. Thank you for trusting me with your health, happiness, and life. And to Rebecca: it's an honor to work with you. Thank you for this opportunity to create together!*

Contents

Our Story *1*

Being the Leader of Your Life *7*

Part 1 **Commitment**

1 Think: Less Is More *15*

2 Set Aside the Time *21*

3 Make It a Routine *27*

4 Commit to Fit *33*

5 Buddy Up *39*

6 Repeat Your Key Messages *43*

Part 2 **Boundaries**

7 Think: Less is More, Revisited *51*

8 Create Ease *55*

9 Eat Well at Social and Work Events *59*

10 Travel in (Fitᴄᴇᴏ) Style *65*

11 Manage Crises, Don't Let Them Manage You *69*

12 Be Agile *75*

13 Recharge Your Batteries *81*

Part 3 **Intention**

14 Mix It Up *89*

15 Navigate Pitfalls and Setbacks *95*

16 Know Your Brand *101*

17 Align Your Stars *107*

18 Slow Down to Speed Up *111*

19 Move to Gain Momentum *115*

Part 4 Self-Care

20 Age Fit, Fit Age *123*

21 Drink the Life Source: H2O *129*

22 Start New Habits for Eating Fit *133*

23 Pay Yourself First *139*

24 Get Your Sleep *143*

25 Keep Good Posture *149*

26 Rest and Recover *155*

Part 5 Heart

27 Strike a Balance *163*

28 Manage Your Energy *171*

29 Be Authentic *179*

30 Make It Fun! *185*

Moving Forward as a Fit CEO *191*

Getting into Your FitCEO Body *193*

Resources *209*

Our Story

Rebecca: Lillian and I met about ten years ago at a San Francisco fitness club, where I am a member and she was a teacher and trainer. It all started when I inquired about using a machine called a Power Plate, which I had seen at a friend's home. My friend said she had discovered this amazing machine in France and that in thirty minutes you could achieve a very effective workout. My San Francisco club had a machine like that, but they said I would have to use it with a trainer. This is how I met Lillian; she was certified on the machine, and she was willing to do thirty-minute sessions with me. We bonded quickly.

Around that time, I had become the head of a business, and this required a long commute three to four days a week, so short sessions and flexibility were key. I met with Lillian, usually two times a month, and as we got to know each other better, we quickly learned that our worldviews about fitness, emotional health, spiritual alignment, and life overall were incredibly in sync, even though we come from different backgrounds.

I was born and raised in San Francisco, and my parents are both medical doctors and Jungian psychoanalysts. I am a fourth-generation San Franciscan/Californian. I have worked in five countries and studied nine languages, and I have been passionate about international business ever since I can remember. As a child, I started my first business, called Rebecca's Little Shop, where I sold "critical" items (like gum, candles, and pot holders) to my family and neighbors. I made many of the products (like the candles and the woven pot holders) in my bedroom. At age thirteen, I got a California business license and expanded into jewelry making, selling jewelry to local stores as well as to friends and family. My business expanded to include distributing my dad's book (*Paddling the Gate*) and, at weekend flea markets, reselling clothing from local stores after the last sale season had ended. I knew early on that I wanted to go into business, and I dreamed about going to business school from the time I was in high school.

I have worked for more than twenty-five years in financial services at Fortune 50 companies and served in roles such as managing director, general manager, president, CEO, and chairman. I have spent most of my time transforming businesses—tuning them up, turning them around, and taking them to the next level. Prior to financial services, I worked as a strategy management consultant in Europe.

Several years ago, I asked Lillian if she would write a book with me on being a fit CEO because fitness, both physical and mental, has been such an integral part of my journey as a leader. When we worked together, Lillian and I connected on so many levels regarding our philosophical approaches to life that I knew we could be great partners for a book project. And she agreed! So here we are now, delivering on a conversation from 2012!

Lillian: I am a Korean-American daughter of Korean immigrants. I was born and raised in the inner city of Chicago. My parents still own a liquor store in a small town just outside the city.

My interest in fitness really started when I was a child.

When I was growing up, extended family members often told me I was fat, too big, and too much. Hearing this led me down a dark path of low self-esteem, body image issues, and eating disorders that began at a young age. I started dieting and working out when I was barely eleven years old. I became very active over time, and through high school, I channeled my energy into sports.

I studied exercise physiology and kinesiology at the University of Illinois at Urbana-Champaign, and throughout college I worked in a shiny new club as a personal trainer and group fitness instructor. I quickly established a successful career in fitness. But in 2007, I hit a glass ceiling and knew I wasn't done growing within the fitness industry.

So, I decided to move out to San Francisco. If I could make it in San Francisco, I could make it anywhere. Between the high cost of living and the competitive fitness industry, I knew I was up for a challenge. I packed my bags, left a thriving business behind, and started all over again in a new city, where I had zero clients.

I applied to work as a personal trainer and group fitness instructor at a high-end club in the heart of San Francisco. After a few years of employment there, I set off on a new leg of my personal and professional journey. It was time to do some personal healing work and deep introspection about where I wanted to take my life next.

After becoming a yoga therapist and an NVC (nonviolent communication) facilitator, I knew I needed to take a path beyond the gym. As I was transitioning into my new integrative coaching practice and business, I met Rebecca. I wasn't planning on taking on new clients at this particular club, but I was willing to work with her because her requests were unique, and they aligned with my situation in many ways.

First, she didn't want traditional personal training. She wanted thirty-minute sessions on equipment that no one else was certified in. Second, she wasn't often in town. This was great because it gave me the space to keep the ball rolling on my next steps in building an integrative coaching business. Third, she was extremely open and easy to work with from day one. This combination led us to build an incredible rapport and trust with each other immediately. I guess you can say we got lucky. That's when experience and timing coincide, or something like that, right?

We spent months, maybe even years, sharing many intimate conversations on everything from health and fitness to relationships and family. We learned that we were so aligned, and we "made a deal" to write a book together one day. Life happened, and we were in touch less often as my transformation coaching business took off and Rebecca ran the banking world. Eight years later, Rebecca called to tell me she was ready to pour her energy into this original agreement, and that's how we ended up here.

My primary intention behind this book is to facilitate a transformation. Being a fit CEO is about showing up for yourself and taking action every day. Taking consistent action is how you become and remain a fit CEO and the leader of your life.

Being the Leader of Your Life

ITCEO IS a book about being the leader of your own life, the boss of *you*. It presents an approach to whole-body fitness—physical, mental, emotional, and spiritual. This book isn't about layering on another demanding routine into your already ambitious schedule. It is about manageably introducing simple, easy, fun habits for total fitness.

Small lifestyle changes can trigger powerful shifts that increase your energy, improve your health, and make life more enjoyable. Busy CEOs and leaders, people starting a new chapter of their life, and people ready to reboot and level up their game can have a complete and whole life—with all the aspects of health, success, and fun—by following the model you'll learn in the pages ahead. We all play multiple roles in our lives, from home to work, from child to parent, from parent to child. *FitCEO* is about how you—as the CEO of a company, a home, or a life—can adopt simple, easy practices and habits for success to become the fit person you want to be, on all levels.

We wrote this book as a quick, fun read on purpose. It is composed of short, pithy chapters, the first sections of which are written by Rebecca. These sections share anecdotes and lessons she's learned from her years of experience integrating healthy habits into her lifestyle as a busy, high-achieving CEO who also happens to be a spouse, mother, sister, and more. In the "immediate and imperfect action" sections that follow, Lillian offers simple steps you can take to move the needle in every area of your life, giving you the tools that will lead to a true transformation. Keep in mind that "immediate" means you start right away, and "imperfect" assures you that you can just start and don't have to worry about being flawless. You will have opportunities to "get in your body," learning exercises and sequences to support physical fitness. And for the "pen to paper" sections, keep a pen and pad or journal close by and write down your notes, thoughts, and commitments. The key with all these exercises: Start. Try them. Make them habits.

In the pages ahead, we provide you with pro tips and knowledge you can use and reuse throughout your day, week, month, year, life. We invite you to approach this book in ways that make integrating the habits of a fit CEO pleasant for you. You could use it as a go-to resource, first reading it from start to finish and then revisiting specific chapters to focus on practices you know you will benefit from and that will improve your life, whether at work or home or while traveling. The book has thirty chapters, so if you're motivated by a challenge, you could read one chapter each day for a month, practicing each chapter's immediate and imperfect action and transforming a new regime into a regular routine. Or you could simply work through the chapters from start to finish, at your own pace. We hope *FitCEO* becomes your constant companion!

The Framework

You'll notice the book is structured in parts that focus on five key elements: commitment, boundaries, intention, self-care, and heart. When, many years ago, we had our one-on-one fitness sessions, our conversations about health and fitness always found their way back to these core themes. So, naturally they emerged again when we sat down to write this book. We think of these elements as pillars that are crucial to success in both work and life. Whenever someone struggles to sustainably maintain health and happiness, it always comes down to one of these pillars being compromised. And without one, the others crumble. You need all five firmly rooted in your life.

First, *commitment*. To be fully integrated, you must commit to paying attention to all the parts of you. This includes a commitment to yourself, your team, your community, and your passions. One of the primary commitments of being a fit CEO is to your physical and emotional fitness, which means putting your health and emotional needs at the same level of importance as your business and family needs. In part 1, we introduce foundational practices for a fit lifestyle and enjoyable ways to bolster your commitment to them.

Boundaries are a critical component of being a fit CEO, too. They can be as simple as stating what's okay and not okay. Boundaries are the key to healthy relationships, keeping your commitments, and maintaining order in your life. Without healthy boundaries, the things that are most important, like self-care, tend to erode. Boundaries keep us honest with ourselves, which ultimately keeps us honest with others and free from much suffering. In part 2, we offer insights about how to know, set, and maintain boundaries for a healthy mind and body—while you travel, under pressure, and in situations where boundaries will surely be tested.

Intention clarifies where you are going and what you want to achieve when you get there. Without intention, you're blowing in the wind. When you have intention, you can arrive at your destination and feel good about your next stop, too. Intention is the ultimate reason you continue to take care of yourself and maintain boundaries. It helps you see the bigger picture when life throws you curveballs. It helps you stay rooted and grounded, with your eyes on the prize. With vision and intention at work, as a leader, you can help others achieve more than what they could achieve alone. And so, in part 3, we explore tools that help you stick with your intentions for success in fitness, in your career, and in your life.

Part 4 centers on *self-care*, looking at simple, powerful ways to make sure you're taking care of *you*. Self-care is not selfish; it is paramount. You must take care of yourself to take care of others, or to lead. Be vigilant in taking care of yourself so you can follow through. You are the one running the household, the business, and every corner of your life. If you are not healthy, well, and happy, everything else can fall apart. If you do not make time for your wellness, you will be forced to take care of your illness. Keep your cup full and let it overflow, making other people's lives much easier and sweeter along the way. You are the arbiter of your happiness.

Lastly, part 5 expands the *heart*. In all things, lead with the heart. Your heart pumps to keep you alive and pours the most vital essence through your body and brain to maintain high function and flow. It is also the epicenter of your soul and the bliss center of your entire being. It's what keeps you moving forward energetically and emotionally. Without heart, you become cold, disconnected, and far from your meaning and purpose. These chapters share lessons to help you be the heart-healthy fit CEO you want to be.

You probably already "know" what to do to get in the driver's seat of your life, especially in the age of information overload and the Internet. The goal of this book is to give you more than information. We want to inspire you to long-lasting and meaningful change through the ethos of "less is more." Transformation is possible, no matter how busy or complex your life might be. We want you to see how simple it can be to be the fit CEO of your life. Read on!

PART ONE

COMMITMENT

1

Think: Less Is More

AVE YOU been brought up in the world of "more is better"? By the end of this book, we hope to persuade you that, in fact, the concept that "less is more" is equally powerful. In many ways, taking this approach can be even more powerful.

In the chapters ahead, you will learn how, in just thirty minutes, three to four times a week, you can feel and be physically fit. What does it mean to feel fit? It means feeling more energetic, more in control of your life, more inspired in everything you do.

Do you often feel tired at the end of a workday, from the physical or mental labor of it, from endless meetings, or from the nonstop barrage of demands on you and your time? Being a fit CEO is not about adding another responsibility to your to-do list. It's about making the most out of your time, doing simple things to feel fit, in little time, enjoyably. This will bring you some "R"—rejuvenation, reinvigoration, restoration, renewal, relaxation—or simply a restart of your mental/physical connection. You choose the R that's best for you now. It is this "reset" that physical exercise can give you, to reinvigorate your energy and to help you rest better at night.

But you do need to invest.

For a minimal cash investment and a few ounces of packing weight, you can get all the equipment you need to be fit anywhere, anytime. And if you don't have the materials that Lillian lists below, no problem. Gravity and movement are free, and in the pages to come, we will show you how to work with them and your environment to get fit, physically and mentally.

Immediate and Imperfect Action

Show up. Do the work. These two steps are everything.

Every rock star, A-player, high performer, and fit CEO I've ever worked with consistently takes these two steps, every single day of their life. No matter what your calling

There is a way
to feel fit, in little
time, enjoyably.

is in life: Show. Up. That literally means to appear—gather the equipment, schedule the workout, follow through on your commitments, and be present.

No matter what you want to accomplish, you have to do the work. There's no other way around it. Some days may be baby steps. Some days will be leaps. As long as you keep moving the needle by 1 percent daily, you're crushing it.

Get in Your Body

You don't need much to get started, but you may want a few tools at your disposal:

- tennis shoes
- workout clothes
- yoga mat
- a jump rope
- short and long resistance bands
- towels
- a chair
- a doorway

PEN TO PAPER

Reflection is an ongoing practice that we'll use throughout this book. In a journal or on a pad of paper or a device, make some notes in response to the following questions:

- How do you want to feel in the next thirty days?
- Why is being a fit CEO important to you?
- What will being a fit CEO do for you?

2

Set Aside the Time

T
HIS BOOK is short for a reason. The belief that
"more is better" has been so deeply ingrained in
our culture that conceiving of and accepting that
"less is more" is next to unfathomable for most of
us when we start out on this journey. But we are determined to prove to you that there is another way.

In chapter 1, you committed to showing up and
doing the work. Maybe you picked up some equipment
or pulled a pair of sweatpants out of the back of your
closet and assessed: *Yes, I have a doorway, I have a
towel, and I have a chair. I'm ready.* So, now what?

Now we are going on a journey together, one step at
a time. No rushing.

For busy CEOs—executives, moms, dads, sisters,
brothers, sons, daughters, friends, employees and

How we spend
our time is how we
value ourselves.

bosses, generalists, and for any and every other role you hold—time is both finite and infinite. In life, time is likely your most precious and scarcest resource. It is also your greatest gift. But there never seems to be "enough" of it. How you spend your time is how you value yourself—and how you live your values. If you value physical fitness, you'll make sure you work exercise and good nutrition into your life. If you value high-quality work, you'll make sure to take your time to focus on the task at hand, to take breaks to refresh your view, and to breathe through distractors that could derail you. And you won't overdo it, either. You'll take exercise, nutrition, and quality work all in moderation so that you enjoy them. So, starting today, the secret is accepting, truly, that less is more.

Are you ready to commit to that? If you truly want more energy, positive thoughts, inspiration, and motivation, part of the package is getting physically fit, and to do that, you've got to set aside the time. Yes, three to four times per week for thirty minutes is a small investment of time that will pay large dividends, for the rest of your life. The gift of time for yourself—for your mental and physical health—is priceless. And it is free.

Immediate and Imperfect Action

Schedule your workouts in your calendar! I always say, "If it isn't on your calendar, it doesn't count." Time is the most valuable asset you have. You can always replace material goods, but you can't replace time. Make room in your schedule for three to four half-hour workouts each week, and then guard and prioritize your calendar to organize around your FitCEO time blocks. Make these sacred. Create the space. Choose times you can commit to no matter what life throws at you or where you are in the world.

And if you miss one of your workout times, don't make it a thing! Find another way to get in your body or recover your time. Here are some ideas:

- Ask if your next one-on-one meeting can be a walk and talk.
- Do some squats while you're waiting for the kettle to boil.
- Schedule three ten-minute walking breaks into your day.
- Give yourself compassion, and schedule in a longer workout the next day.

PEN TO PAPER

Reflect on the commitment to scheduling your thirty-minute workouts three to four times per week:

- How would you like to spend your blocks of time?
- What will you give care and attention to?
- What will be the ripple effect of staying committed to your time blocks?
- How will you feel after you show up to your time blocks?
- Why is it important for you to feel this way?

3

Make It a Routine

ARE YOU in? Are you ready to get hooked?

In the last chapter, Lillian talked about scheduling your workouts. Now, I can already hear your resistance, saying, *Yeah, but do you know how busy I am? It's not that simple . . .*

I'm here to tell you: it *is* simple. You can travel every week for your job; you can work at home and be swamped all day; you can work in your own area out of the home or on video and feel you have no time—but you do! The key? You must *schedule the time* with yourself.

Sometimes this requires looking for "hidden" blocks of time, as well as some creative thinking. You might slot in a thirty-minute workout after checking into your hotel and before your business dinner, or you might plan a break between work and dinner. (Even if you go back to work after dinner, you'll benefit from that short burst of physical activity!) Prefer mornings? Then schedule the time in your calendar, three to four times per week, before breakfast or your first commitment of the day. (Remember to include the transition time that you need to get from your room to your dinner, to shower and change, and so on.) The key is scheduling the time for a short exercise sequence in your room, in the gym, on the sidewalk, in the yard, or anywhere with a little space: a garden, a park, a basement . . . You get the idea!

To make something a habit, you need to do it for thirty days. In fact, according to different studies, it can take 21 to 284 days to create a routine. Phillippa Lally's study published in the *European Journal of Social Psychology* notes that, depending on the difficulty of the task, forming a habit can take, on average, sixty-six days. A simple habit may take twenty-one days to embed; a more complex habit takes more time.

In my experience, getting hooked on a thirty-minute exercise routine means doing it regularly for thirty days. If thirty minutes feels like too much, begin with a ten-minute fitness routine, three to four days a week. This is a simpler task on the scale of complexity. Build this time up to thirty minutes in increments. Make the

Make it so enjoyable that, within approximately thirty days, you feel a "call to exercise"—you crave that healthy hit of endorphins.

activity so enjoyable that, within approximately thirty days, you'll feel a "call to exercise"—you'll crave that healthy endorphin hit.

Yep, after a month, if you are like most humans, you will be hooked on exercise.

Immediate and Imperfect Action

Name it to claim it. Once you've created space on your calendar, name those times so they have more energy and power behind them. You are more likely to show up for yourself when you are specific and intentional about how you want to use that time.

What are all the ways you like to move or break a sweat? Name your space with the physical practice you want to show up for. Here are some ideas:

- Hills and Stairs
- Dance Party
- Strength Session
- Yoga and Chill
- Cardio Circuit

Get in Your Body

Once you've committed physical exercise to your schedule, work with what's available to you, and focus on the primary intention of spending time connecting with your body. There are many ways to get into your body, from walking to dance to sports to yoga and more. You can also design a sequence of movements that can be done anywhere. Here's how.

The general framework consists of

- warm-up/stretching
- upper-body work
- lower-body work
- cardio
- core work
- cooldown/stretching

Do two exercises in each of the above categories, performing the movements for one to two minutes each. Repeat the cycle of upper- and lower-body work, cardio, and core work three times, taking breaks as needed. Check out "Getting into Your FitCEO Body" at the back of the book (see page 193) for some basic instructions on these movements, as well as a few more exercises in each category. Here is an example set:

Warm-Up

- child's pose
- side-to-side stretch

Cardio

- jump rope
- jumping jacks

Upper-Body Work

- seated rows
- push-ups

Core

- bridge pose
- forearm plank

Lower-Body Work

- squats
- alternating lunges

(Repeat upper- and lower-body work, cardio, and core three times in a circuit.)

Cooldown

- downward dog
- kneeling low lunge

This thirty-minute set offers one example. As you become familiar with it, you can mix and match exercises to suit you. Just make sure you hit all those areas—and don't shirk on the warm-up or cooldown.

4

Commit to Fit

AM A disciplined person; that is part of how I became a successful executive. However, staying fit with a busy schedule—with a spouse, kids, work, travel, community, spirituality, friends, chores, and all that goes into a whole life—takes commitment. For me, keeping the commitment to health requires habitual discipline.

Through repetition and commitment, I have developed habits to support my fitness. When I arrive somewhere after a long flight or drive, I go for a walk right after I drop off my bags in my room. If it is nighttime, then I at least stretch and get the blood moving after having sat for so many hours. I often return calls while I walk—that is such a great way to move and also get through my to-do list.

Keeping the commitment to health requires habitual discipline.

Everyone at work knows that I walk or work out most days, too. My colleagues and team members have learned that I need a break before we book a dinner or a meeting in the evening. When that's not possible, most are willing to have a walking meeting with me or go for a stroll after a business dinner. I have seen many a square and park—from Moscow to Hong Kong to Montevideo! My colleagues have told me they now travel with sneakers because of my consistent walking—before or after a meeting, or going on foot to dinner and skipping the taxi or Uber.

These are commitments I make to myself: If I can add a walk, I do it. If I can see an interesting site en route to a meeting by walking a few blocks out of my way, I do it. Not only am I more physically fit because of it, but I also get to see more of the amazing cities I travel to around the world, instead of just seeing the inside of an office building, a hotel, a car, and a plane. Seeing a bit of the world when I travel on business nourishes my soul.

Immediate and Imperfect Action

Work for fifty-two minutes, break for seventeen.

This advice follows data gathered by the productivity app DeskTime, which tracks the computer use of employees. Its data show that the highest-performing 10 percent of work happens in segments of fifty-two consecutive minutes of work, followed by seventeen-minute breaks.

Get up from your desk every fifty-two minutes (or every hour) for a quick walk or stretch, or just to breathe deeply. Moving the body gets the blood pumping and oxygen flowing through your body and brain, which will amplify productivity when you're back at your desk.

Get in Your Body

Try these simple arm raises timed to your breath:

- Stand up.
- Inhale through your nose as you reach your arms up overhead.
- Exhale through your nose as you pull your elbows down into a scarecrow position.
- Reach up again as you inhale.
- Pull your elbows down to scarecrow position as you exhale.
- Repeat this movement twenty times.

PEN TO PAPER

Write a statement that addresses these questions:

- What are you willing to commit to for the next thirty days so you can build your fitness?
- How will you benefit from this commitment?
- How will this ripple into other areas of your life?
- What is the cost of putting off this commitment?

5

Buddy Up

S OME OF the best ways to keep a commitment are, first, to write it down and, second, to tell someone about it: a friend or two or more, or a family member. Even more powerful is to get a "buddy" to commit with you and do the activity together.

When COVID-19 shelter-in-place orders began in March 2020 to "flatten the curve," my sister and I decided to go for a walk after working from home. Given that our gyms were closed, we thought we'd explore our city by foot. We started walking toward each other around 5 p.m., met at around 5:15, and selected a path. We live in San Francisco, a city with lots of parks and views, so we alternated our walks in the Presidio and Golden Gate Park. What was great was that no matter if it was cold or foggy or if we were tired, we each texted each other around five o'clock:

"getting my shoes on"
 or
"see you shortly."

Even if one of us felt lazy, we kept our commitment. My sister said to me one day: "I'm losing weight with all this walking!" She added, "This is so great. I know you'll show up, so I show up, and we have our mental and physical break from 'work from home'!"

At this writing, my sister and I have walked together most Mondays to Fridays for more than ten months. And I walk with a friend on the weekends. Buddying up is a motivator and adds fuel to commitment. Who do you want to buddy up with for your thirty minutes a day? Even if you do your routine in separate spaces, doing it with a friend can give you a boost. Accountability works! Accountability is one of the keys to commitment.

Immediate and Imperfect Action

Make the first move. Being the leader of your life often means taking the necessary steps to set yourself up for

This is so great.
I know you'll show
up, so I show up!

success. Reach out and find someone willing to buddy up with you. You will be amazed at how many people would love to go on a morning walk, attend lunchtime yoga, or meet you for a workout instead of happy hour.

PEN TO PAPER

Reflect on how a buddy could ramp up your accountability:

- What would you like a buddy for?
- What do you need accountability for?
- Write a list of colleagues, friends, or family members you connect with regularly. Of those people, who would you like to move with?

Reach out and ask your people to commit to a regular schedule with you.

Repeat Your Key Messages

6

AS A leader, I have observed that when I want a message to get out to the team, building it into the team's DNA takes extensive repetition. Years back, I read an article that said that in large, complex organizations, a message must be repeated twenty times before it makes it from the leader to the front line. So, I have learned to practice repetition of key messages.

The most profound and lasting change I have undertaken is transforming a business's culture. To do that, I first introduced the new culture. Then I explained the motivation for the change. Following that, I discussed the desired shift in the company's behaviors and habits; I

Mantra: I am committed to my growth and well-being.

brought this up in meetings throughout the organization, from board meetings to monthly and weekly town hall, all-team meetings. I then used the pillars of the culture (the client, the employee, the shareholder, and operational excellence) to drive the routines of the business.

Being a fit leader involves the same patterns of embedding the reasons for the change (aka, the motivation) and the routines that support it (aka, the behaviors and habits). It involves not only physical health but also mental and spiritual fitness. As the leader of your own life, you can make your healthy practices your go-to mindset! Affirmations, or mantras, can help with that.

One affirmation I have used a lot is for public speaking. Before I get up in front of a large crowd, I tell myself, "I have a message of importance, and people want to hear what I have to say." I say this to myself multiple times before I take the stage, and I also write "smile" and "look up" on each page of my speech. With these mantras and reminders, I have become a very relaxed speaker over the years. These days, I no longer need to consciously repeat the mantras, as they have become part of my DNA, an embedded habit.

Repetition is powerful. When you hear something multiple times, like the chorus of your favorite song, it sticks in your head. (You might even walk around singing it to yourself.)

Immediate and Imperfect Action

Use affirmations. These are positive statements that declare what you are setting out to do or who you want to be. They are extremely powerful in transforming the way you view yourself and your capabilities. Whether you are preparing your child for a high school musical or getting ready for a big presentation, affirmations will help you believe in yourself and act confidently.

Repetition is how we build muscle memory! Create affirmations and repeat them to yourself ten times every morning to bolster your commitment to your FitCEO routine. As I prepare for my day, I write my affirmations down so I can see them. The act of writing the affirmations embeds them in me until they become ingrained, a part of my automatic memory. Try this for thirty days to build your habit.

PEN TO PAPER

Write one to three affirmations that align with your goals, how you want to feel, or who you want to be. Omit the words *won't*, *don't*, *try*, and *not* when crafting your affirmations. Use clear, action-oriented, and affirmative language in the present or future tense.

Here are some examples of what *not* to do:

- I will try to work out and reflect on my actions this week.
- I will try to drink a lot of water this week.
- I don't want to be weak or set a bad example for the people in my life.
- I will try to be compassionate in everything I do.
- I will not be impatient with my team this week.
- I won't do things that distract me from my growth and well-being.

Here is how to rewrite them to be effective and transformative:

- I will show up every day to care for my physical and mental health.

- I will drink sixty-four ounces of water every day this week.
- I am powerful and influential, and I set an example for the people in my life.
- I have compassion in everything I do, from self-care to leading my team.
- I will be patient and caring with my team this week.
- I am committed to my growth and well-being.

BONUS

Integrate affirmations into your routines:

- Schedule affirmations to go off in your phone every hour.
- Write affirmations on sticky notes and place them by your desk.
- Set an affirmation that resonates as your screensaver on your phone.
- Use affirmations as passwords on your computer.
- Keep a mini chalkboard by your bathroom mirror and write a new affirmation for each month.

PART TWO

BOUNDARIES

7

Think: Less Is More, Revisited

WHY A second chapter on the topic of "less is more"? Because this topic is the most counterintuitive. And because "less is more" is about truly listening to what is okay for you. It is a belief system.

When we started our work together, Lillian would regularly say to me, "Less can often be more." My background and training is all about "more is more," so I honestly struggled with this one. Over the years, though, I have learned the power of this position. Think about it. From business memos to meetings, there is power in simplicity. One page or less is usually better than a multi-page memo that people don't feel they have time to read; meeting for twenty-five minutes is usually better than meeting for thirty; a fifty-minute meeting is better than an hour-long one. Rest can be the best thing, sometimes.

I have often noticed that if I lack sleep, I gain weight and feel drained. When we sleep, our bodies repair themselves, so less exercise and more sleep can sometimes be the answer. Less can be more when working on a project, including an exercise project. My sister and I noticed that as our COVID-19 shelter-in-place time was extended, our walks got longer, and soon I was having knee pain. I changed my shoes and rested, but then we went back to shorter walks, and voila: no knee pain and more energy. Sometimes too much exercise or too much of anything can drain or literally injure you.

Back in our training sessions, when Lillian and I lifted weights or did other exercises, we often used shorter "sprints" versus longer ones, and we met for thirty minutes instead of the typical fifty-minute session. I would always leave the sessions with energy, not drained and tired. This was key for me because I was going home to my family, and I wanted energy for my kids and husband!

Over the years, I heard many teams ask how we could have fewer meetings. A core practice I implemented

Taking things off
your calendar is
a power move.

was that whenever we wanted to add a regular, recurring meeting, we had to take a different meeting off the calendar. Over time, this made us review our regular meetings, which we typically did every four to six months, to see if they were still helping us drive the areas we needed in order to achieve our goals. This practice is so important: when you add something to a full calendar, you must take something off to make room.

The beauty of this habit, of taking things off your calendar, is that it allows you to honor your commitment to yourself and your boundaries while really listening to yourself and your team or your family.

Immediate and Imperfect Action

Take something *off* your calendar.

Yes, I know this sounds so counterintuitive! Sometimes, it isn't about *adding* more to our plates to get better results. Reducing your load and saying no can be incredibly liberating. It can bring the clarity you need when making hard decisions and prevent emotional and mental burnout.

Taking things off your calendar is a power move.

8

Create Ease

HONORING YOURSELF requires honoring your boundaries. Knowing what you do and don't want is essential. I know, for instance, that when I travel, I need a way to safely move or work out at my hotel. Over the years, I have learned to choose hotels that have a gym, a pool, or a walking path nearby to make it easy to move for thirty minutes. I always leave my tennis shoes, my resistance bands and jump rope kit, and a swimsuit packed in my suitcase. I repack my workout clothes each time I travel. I exercise before breakfast or dinner. Those are the "sweet spots" in my calendar. If I am in a complete jam because of board meetings and overly packed schedules, then I try to walk to meetings, or I request a walking meeting.

Sometimes I have to remember to just pause ... sit ... do nothing ... and clear my mind.

I also have learned over the years to take breaks. If my body is just too tired, I don't work out. I rest, truly. This is one of the hardest things for me to do—recognize my own boundaries with exercise. I am so hooked on it that I have to consciously permit myself *not* to do it. It helps for me to remember that rest is a critical part of total fitness.

I practice honoring my boundaries by making it easy to rest. Sometimes I have to remember to just pause... sit... do nothing... and clear my mind. I have designated "triggers" to do this: for instance, when I was flying three to four times a month, I would use the take-off time to look out the window or close my eyes and rest. I also tried to do this before a business dinner or on my way home from the office. Designating "triggered calm" or "empty mind" times made rest an easier habit and allowed me to show up more fully for whatever encounter came next—with family, friends, or colleagues.

Immediate and Imperfect Action

Pause and take three deep breaths.

When life is going a hundred miles per hour, you may not even realize when you've reached your limit.

Connecting with your breath instantly brings you back into your body. Whenever you notice your energy, thoughts, or emotions being pulled in multiple directions, simply take a moment to inhale and exhale deeply through your nose. All you need is three breath cycles to regroup and get in touch with your true state.

PEN TO PAPER

Reflect on your energy levels:

- How do you feel on a scale of 1 to 10, with 1 being super-tired and 10 being super-energized?
- Based on your rating, what does your body need?

If you are exhausted and you know you've been burning the candle at both ends, find some time to recharge. If you are feeling energized and have energy to burn, put on your workout clothes and break a sweat!

9

Eat Well at Social and Work Events

SOCIAL AND work dinners and events can present a challenge to maintaining a fit, healthy routine! After all, not much zaps the fun, energizing benefits of a simple workout routine like overindulging in dehydrating alcohol and rich, non-nutritious food. I employ many tactics—each works at different times. Bottom line: be kind to yourself, and be realistic.

One tip for success is not to arrive at events hungry. If I am hungry before going to a dinner, I try to eat an apple. Most hotels now keep bowls of apples at the front desk or in the workout room or store.

I enjoy wine, and at a work dinner, although I do not decline to have a drink with others, I almost always simultaneously order a glass of sparkling water. This way, I drink both water and wine, and I stick with water until the food arrives. So, usually, while others are on their second glass, I am still on my first. Let's face it: two glasses of alcohol before dinner makes it pretty hard to maintain any form of discipline. I may have a second glass at dinner, but if I do, I order a half-glass (and always continue with my water as well). I am five foot one, so there is not a lot of room in me for more than one and a half glasses of wine.

I also have a fairly strict routine of ordering a salad, with dressing on the side, or vegetable soup as my starter. For the main course, I choose grilled fish and vegetables. I love spice and sauce to keep it interesting. For dessert I usually order fruit salad, fresh fruit, or a sorbet. And, yes, I indulge in bread, but I try to keep it to one piece or so.

That is the basic outline of how I eat at a restaurant or social gathering. If it is a buffet, I generally choose the vegetarian fare. I love trying different things, so I will sample various foods, but in moderation. If I nibble on passed hors d'oeuvres, then I skip the bread and butter at dinner. My mantra is: *moderation—it's okay to try, just don't overdo it.*

The key is to *enjoy* the event and not focus on the food.

I learned one other useful strategy from a former colleague: think of work dinners as being about the people or the experience, *not* about the food. So, the menu is not the main event. It is a way to catch up with friends, colleagues, and clients or to meet new people. When I approach an event this way, the food is much less important because I am there for a higher purpose. The key is to *enjoy* the experience and not focus on the food. Slow down, talk, and soon your plate will be taken away, perhaps before you have even finished!

Immediate and Imperfect Action

Focus on your primary intention. Whenever you are out of your usual routine or environment, falling off track is all too easy. That is why it's so important to be intentional with everything you do. Before you become a victim of late dinners and social events, recall your original vision and intention for your fitness and health.

PEN TO PAPER

When you know you'll be in a situation that will challenge your all-round health and fitness routine, reflect on your intentions with questions like:

- What is the purpose of this meal?
- What is the intention behind this happy hour?
- What is your desired outcome for attending this dinner?

10

Travel in (FitCEO) Style

PLANES, TRAINS, automobiles. Travel for work can impinge on your boundaries, testing your resolve to move regularly, eat well, rest fully, and more. But travel can also be the playground for your intention to be fit. There are many barriers to exercise and overall healthy choices when on the road, but there are also just as many "hacks" to make it work.

One of the most important things you can do is drink lots of water when traveling, because airplanes and air conditioning dehydrate you, and that will make you tired.

Getting your steps in is a good way to stay active on a trip. The flight to Singapore from San Francisco is a sixteen-hour direct route. On that trip and others like it, I walk the aisles as much as possible and move every

Walk the hallways of the airport.

hour that I am not sleeping. When sitting, I do several small movements: wriggling my toes, squeezing my muscles into tension and then relaxing them, and moving my arms (without hitting my neighbor!). I often occupy the space next to the door by the kitchen area, befriending the flight attendants who let me stretch there for ten minutes when there is no turbulence. On flights to China, sometimes there are double-decker seats, and I walk the stairs.

If the airplane itself is your zone-out place, have no fear. You can walk the hallways of the airport. I use the time between my arrival at the airport and the boarding call to walk the halls of the airport with my rolling bag. I often get a thirty-minute walk in before a flight! And if you are flying through Heathrow, wear tennis shoes because, no matter what, you will walk for at least thirty minutes to get through security and passport control and to the baggage claim area.

When I arrive at my destination, I lie on the floor of my hotel room with my head on a pillow and my legs up the wall, reversing the blood flow in my legs. In yoga, this is considered a restorative pose. For me, it does two things: it eases jet lag and stops my ankles from swelling. It's a win-win, and it is super-relaxing.

Immediate and Imperfect Action

Dress for success. If you stay ready, you don't have to get ready. When traveling, wear something you can comfortably move and stretch in.

Get in Your Body

As soon as you arrive at your hotel room, drop off your bags and go out for a quick walk around the area. When you get back to your room, throw your legs up the wall like Rebecca does, and/or do a quick set of stretches. You can find instructions on how to perform these stretches in the section "Getting into Your Fitceo Body," which begins on page 193. Here's a sequence to try:

- child's pose
- happy baby
- bridge pose
- supine twists
- knees to chest
- downward dog

11

Manage Crises, Don't Let Them Manage You

CRISES COME up. They are inevitable, and they are the ultimate crashers of your staying-fit party. Crises come in all sizes—small and medium and truly enormous—and at home, at work, and in communities, globally. We have all lived through many. The key is to manage your response to crises, treating your mental, physical, and emotional health as a sacred boundary not to be worn down by your response to whatever trouble you're facing.

Some people tend to approach crises through a fact-based, analytic lens, and others might have a highly personal, emotional response. In all cases, crises can be overwhelming. They make us feel as though we are under attack, and the natural response, built right into our DNA, is to go into fight-or-flight mode. Knowing how to respond in this state is vital. In a critical situation, you want to be able to shift from a reactive, fearful stance to a perspective of curiosity and openness about the calamity. Stepping back, breathing, then breathing again more deeply is helpful. When a crisis occurs, breathe deeply and evenly for a few minutes, then look at the situation again, through a calmer lens.

Once you have some perspective, assess the problem and determine what you need. Often, more information is required before you can decide on a course of action. If that is the case, then get the information, calling in experts or pulling a team together, if you need to, to do this. Remain calm, and plan. Use breathing as a tool to keep your cool.

This technique will help you with discernment, too. Some crises truly are big ones—a major market fluctuation, the loss of a big client, an illness in the family, and the like. For crises of leadership and slow-forming health problems, you can step back and plan your course of action. Of course, some crises, like a literal fire you need to put out, do require an "auto-response."

But don't mistake the smaller crises—late airplanes, a missed meeting, skipping a meal, a slight oversight by a member of your team, and so on—for disasters. You can still determine how you respond to a minor mess by breathing deeply, taking a longer view on the issue, and giving yourself or someone else a break—these kinds of situations are literally not the end of the world. Appreciate the context: if it is out of your control, like the late airplane, then relax into it, and know it's out of your hands. If it is a crisis of your making (overreacting or overeating/overdrinking, for example), then label it a gift of insight, and learn from it. How do you want to address such a mini-crisis next time? You will build up a strong set of muscles, because all of these mini-stresses will help you through the bigger ones.

I remember clearly the day I learned to become calm when things are out of my control. I was in New York City waiting for my flight home to SFO, and I was sitting near the counter where clients were asking for help from the airline employees. I watched person after person approach one agent and literally scream, yell, bully, and harass her about the late flight—when was it taking off, what was happening? I watched adults of all ages turn bright red and look like their heads might explode.

I decided, then and there, that I would try never to be like that. I walked up to the agent afterward and said, "Wow, you must be so stressed after all those attacks. I just wanted to say I noticed, and I hope your day gets better." She smiled, appreciative of the recognition.

Some years, I have flown more than three hundred thousand miles, and at times I have sat at airports waiting for delayed planes for twelve hours. I've ended up traveling three days to get to an event that's a five-hour flight away. I take one step at a time and know that the situation is not in my control, but I can control how I respond. I take positive action to address the circumstances and get to my destination, even if I'm late. I do not give up, and I do not hurt my body with excess stress!

Immediate and Imperfect Action

Practice gratitude. When we are in a state of crisis, we get stressed out, spiral out of control, and snap at others, and we can fall into victim mentality very quickly. Being in a state of gratitude is the literal opposite of victim mentality. You can't be grateful and feel sorry for

I take one step at a time and know that the situation is not in my control, but I can control how I respond.

yourself at the same time. It is energetically impossible to be in both states at once.

The next time you find yourself spiraling into negativity over things that are out of your control, shift to gratitude. It puts things into perspective pretty quickly and may prevent you from saying or doing something harmful.

PEN TO PAPER

What are you grateful for and why? Start a gratitude journal. Every day, write down at least five things you are grateful for. It will change your life!

BONUS

Send gratitude out! Text or email three people to tell them why you are grateful for them. Some starting points:

- What do they bring into your life?
- What is the difference they make in your life?
- How do they help you feel supported and seen?

12

Be Agile

NIMBLENESS AND agility are key strengths in business. These qualities also show you where your boundaries are and when you are willing to stretch them, or not.

When I was asked to express in one word what I had learned from my first six months of COVID-19 and working from home, I thought and responded: *flexibility*. I would have thought I was pretty nimble already, but sheltering in place and moving all meetings to video taught me a lot about flexibility and agility. I was used to agile thinking in digital scrum teams with six-week sprints to release a new mobile feature, for instance. But during the pandemic, I soon learned that different kinds of agility and flexibility were equally important.

We all wobble,
but we don't
have to fall down.

Suddenly, we were "meeting" in each other's bedrooms, kitchens, and guest rooms, with children, spouses, roommates, and pets wandering on-screen sometimes. I still had boundaries, but I had to stretch and be more flexible about them. I also learned that I had to let go of schedule changes and just "flow" with the ever-changing times of meetings and canceled trips.

We all wobble, but we don't have to fall down. Having solid roots with flexible limbs allows us to bend without breaking. In this respect, two analogies have served me well throughout my career: seaweed and martial arts. When in a "storm" at work, I try to remember that I am like seaweed, which has strong roots in the ocean floor and yet is extremely flexible as each wave hits. I can bounce back after each wave, still solid with my roots. Aikido uses a similar metaphor: you use the force of your attacker to deflect their energy and move into a safe position. I have used these metaphors to handle stress from the front line to the boardroom, navigating challenging situations and remaining agile and flexible.

Another great tool for agility and flexibility comes from the improvisation technique. In improv, you are taught to say yes to anything another actor says and then add to that yes, moving the scene forward. This

is a powerful way to take the energy from a real or per-
ceived attack and use it to move a dialogue forward, no
matter how stressful. This is also powerful at home
with partners, spouses, children, and friends: instead
of responding with a no, try an emphatic "Yes! And..."
Saying "Yes, and...," you can draw a line to mark your
limits and still allow yourself to be open and pervious.

Immediate and Imperfect Action

Feel your feet on the ground. Get grounded, and create more flow as a result. The more you are rooted and
grounded in your body, the better you can respond
to tension building in it. The more you are rooted and
grounded in your mind, the better you can respond to
the curveballs of life.

Get in Your Body

Use yoga poses as a metaphor for how you want to show
up in life. These postures will help you get grounded and
open at the same time:

- **Bridge pose:** In this pose, you are supine, with your feet and shoulders pressed firmly into the floor. Engage your abdominals and glutes as you lift your hips off the floor. The posture is grounding and opens the heart at the same time, teaching you to be firm in who you are and what you believe in while being compassionate to the ever-changing demands of work, home, and life.

- **Kneeling low lunge:** This posture is grounding and stabilizing. It also creates more flexibility and mobility in the hips, which can become tight from long hours of sitting at a desk or on an airplane. Is there any area of your life that needs more grounding and stabilization? Is there any area of your life where you can be more flexible?

- **Figure-four glute stretch:** This posture is grounding and wonderful for releasing tension in the glutes and hips. When we are under pressure and stress, we don't even realize how much we clench! This position allows you to release and relax the parts of you that get the most wound up. Instructions for this stretch can be found in the section "Getting into Your FitCEO Body."

13

Recharge
Your Batteries

RECOVERY AND renewal are all parts of staying fit—mentally, physically, and spiritually. How each of us does this varies. For me, adventure and vacations recharge and energize me. Daily walks and fresh air are vital for me to refresh. And in moments of stress, I just walk outside, even if only for a minute, to look at the sky. Each of us needs breaks; each of us needs to unplug. (Literally, yes—unplug the devices!) At night, I do not bring the phone into the bedroom with me. I don't want to see the blue light of it charging or look at the screen. The phone is plugged in, in a different room, but it is unplugged from me!

Renewal is so powerful and can take many forms. Time off is a big one. Many people don't think they can take time off. *You can!* It is always okay to take time off for yourself. It will make you a better person, and if you lead a business, you will be role modeling for your team how critical taking time off is. *Do it!*

I married into a European family and learned early on that vacations are sacred. I met my husband in Paris. In France, the country practically shuts down in August, as many offices close, and the French take three to four weeks off.

Throughout my career, when I took vacations, I left different folks in charge and distributed the responsibility of running different meetings among the team. People could always call me if something urgent came up, but over the years I was called only three times while on vacation: once because my attendance was needed at an emergency board meeting, once because an employee was giving notice, and once because a merger deal came through. In more than thirty years of working and taking vacations, that is a rate of one call per ten years! When I became CEO of a business and took vacations, I checked emails once a day, in the morning, and then put my work phone in the safe of my hotel room

Many people don't think they can take time off. *You can!*

so I could not see emails coming through all day. I truly unplugged!

In most cases, my team grew and learned to cooperate better when they had to make decisions without me. I also showed the team that *they* had permission to take vacations, and they too were recharged when they came back. A former boss once even told me that after watching me take three weeks off every year and seeing that the business did not fail—in fact, my team gained in maturity and ability when I left them in charge—he decided he too could take vacations! Wow. So, I not only role modeled for my team but also for my managers that vacations are good and effective.

Taking breaks is a gift to yourself, your family, your friends, and your team. For you, it may be camping, or a walk on the beach, or a big trip abroad. Whatever recharges you, make sure you unplug. Recuperation will power you through difficult times. We can all take a page from the Europeans' book and learn about enjoying our lives—working to live versus living to work! Give yourself permission to recharge. It pays huge dividends in all areas of your life. Think of it as time "to be" and not time "to do."

Immediate and Imperfect Action

Give yourself mini-breaks by routinely shutting off your devices and unplugging with intention.

My brother, who is in IT, says that most of the problems his clients face are fixed when he asks this simple question: "Have you tried turning it off and back on again?" You work the same way.

Here are some benefits to turning yourself off and back on. You can

- recharge your energy
- refocus your mind
- reset your mood
- renew your sense of purpose
- reconnect to your joy

Get in Your Body

You can also take breaks throughout your day. Try this:

- Take a seat and close your eyes.

- Inhale and exhale deeply through your nose three times.

- Roll your shoulders backward twenty times.

- Roll your shoulders forward twenty times.

- Roll your head and neck around clockwise slowly five times. (If rolling your neck is bothersome, simply turn your head to the right and then to the left. Drop your chin toward your chest, and tilt your head back to look up toward the sky. Breathe naturally through your nose as you stretch in each direction slowly and carefully.)

- Roll your head and neck around counterclockwise slowly five times.

PEN TO PAPER

Reflect on these questions:

- How can you unplug for ten minutes every day this week?
- What are you allowing and not allowing by placing these boundaries? What will your breaks protect?
- How will this benefit you?

PART THREE

INTENTION

14

Mix It Up

ONE KEY to staying engaged in fitness—and life—is variety. Another is consistency.

I consistently block time in my schedule for movement. I also build in "serial consistency" when I travel. For instance, when I travel to warm climates, I bring a swimsuit and swim for thirty minutes a day. When I travel in the winter, I walk or do my thirty-minute routine with bands or a jump rope, and if the hotel has a gym, I may use its equipment and do a half-hour elliptical session. I like to mix it up to keep it engaging, keep me mentally fresh, and avoid boredom with a particular workout. On vacation, I vary it more by playing tennis, swimming, walking on beaches, or hiking in the mountains.

When you deny or
override your feelings,
that is when you get
burned out, injured,
or sick.

Prevent yourself from getting into a rut. You have options and can mix it up. I love to dance, and if a dance class works with my schedule when I am at home, I am there. I usually take dance classes two to four times a month, and for me they are pure joy, combining music and fitness. I also love kickboxing, and I take a class a few times a month whenever I am not on the road. And guess what? These routines all started in my thirties, when I had just had two babies and could spare only ten minutes a day. Anything is possible. Your only constraint is your will. You *can* do it!

Just as it is with exercise, and with life in general, in business no one wants a routine to go stale. Mix it up there, too. Even if set routines serve you well, take a break from them to step back, get a bird's-eye view, and revisit your intentions and purpose with them. Mixing them up could be refreshing for the team, as well. I often used off-sites, deep dives, or celebrations of milestones to switch up routines, and I included forms of recognition so that others could see shifts and be energized by acknowledging how far we had come to realize our shared vision.

Immediate and Imperfect Action:

Get in touch with your feelings. One of the biggest road-blocks my clients face is "task mentality." Instead, truly listen to your body for what it needs. It is constantly giving you cues, signals, and feedback.

Rather than doing a particular workout because you "have to" or are "supposed to," listen to your body—is that aching shoulder telling you that you need to stretch rather than break a sweat? Are your tight hips saying, "Shake me! Dance!" rather than, "Go for a run today"? Or is an overall dull, listless feeling telling you that you need to move around and boost your heart rate for at least twenty minutes? Your body has its special ways of speaking to you. Trust that it knows what to do. When you deny or override your feelings, that is when you get burned out, injured, or sick.

Get in Your Body

Follow this formula, filling in the blanks with the options below.

If you feel _____, do this: _____

- tight / stretch, yoga, dance

- achy / take an Epsom salt bath or book a massage

- sad / go upside down (with a bridge, a downward dog, or another inversion, like legs up the wall)

- sluggish / go for a walk or take a cold shower

- anxious / take five deep breaths, go for a jog, and write it out

- restless / kickbox, rock climb, play a sport, break a sweat

15

Navigate Pitfalls and Setbacks

VIEW LIFE as a dance. We move forward, we move back, we move sideways. We move. The good news: we generally move forward over time! Intention drives us forward, but there are always setbacks, pits, or bumps along the way. Some of the hardest for me happened when I was traveling week over week across multiple time zones and I was just plain old tired. I would work my ten-to-twelve-hour days and then board a flight home from the East Coast or a foreign country. When I was tired, it was so hard not to just eat whatever was put in front of me and say yes to all the nuts, wine, salt, and junk food the flight attendants had on offer. So, I made a deal with myself: if I was flying at night or on a weekend, I limited my work to two hours so that I had time to relax over dinner and a movie or a book. If I was flying during business hours, then I usually worked. I also treated myself to a sundae, or whatever felt like a treat, when I wanted one, because I was spending so much of my life in the air. But if I wanted the ice cream, I didn't have the bread, and so on. I took breaks, but I was strategic about it so that I didn't regret it the next day!

The moral of the story: be nice to yourself, without overdoing it.

Some of the worst bumps in travel happen when you get stuck for a long time at the airport because of canceled flights, bad weather, and so on. I once had an important trip to Puebla, Mexico, to receive a Lifetime Achievement Award from the Fulbright Association. At the ceremony, I was to give a speech to the three hundred event attendees. I left on a Wednesday so that I would arrive relaxed and early and have time to meet with clients before Friday's ceremony. But on that trip, my four traveling companions and I experienced all manner of delays, from mechanical malfunction to acts of God. It was insane.

Sometimes, when life throws crazy curveballs at you, the best action is to create space to let things play out. Let go of the outcome.

The first night, after sitting in the airport for hours, we had to find a hotel at 2 a.m. after the airline told us that because of ice storms, the airport had to be shut down. The next day, the plane for our rebooked flight blew out a tire during the taxi for takeoff. So, we left hours later but could only get to Mexico City. The five of us then rented a small van and drove to Puebla, arriving on Friday, just hours before the main event! On this occasion, I did not worry about food and exercise. I just went with the flow and tried to laugh at the insanity of it all. My mother and son had left a day after me, and they arrived in Puebla on Thursday! In the end, though, it all worked out, and it was a fun story to tell the award-ceremony guests.

We all had an intention: to get to Puebla for my award, through ice, snow, and sleet, and we shifted from planes to cars to buses to get there. Without such commitment to the vision of our end goal, lesser souls would have given up!

Immediate and Imperfect Action

Create space and let go. Change and uncertainty are guaranteed in life. Sometimes, when life throws crazy curveballs at you, the best action is to allow for space to let things play out. Let go of the outcome. Accept the present moment, and trust in the perfection of now.

Get in Your Body

Close your eyes and take three deep breaths. Visualize all the moving parts of your life growing a little extra space between them. Invite in the unexpected with ease, and allow yourself to embody the sensation of letting go.

PEN TO PAPER

Write this affirmation ten times: "I trust the process. I trust myself. I trust that this moment is perfect exactly as it is."

16

Know Your Brand

ART OF leading a team or running a business includes not only your company's brand but also your personal brand, your strengths, and your vision of yourself. When I entered the workforce, I quickly learned that everyone has a brand, whether it's consciously built or not. I did not consciously build mine, but people often reflected on my style and attributes: high-energy, passionate, engaged, and professional. My brand evolved over time as I took on more responsibility and signed on to solve difficult problems, from "turnaround" to "turn-it-up" opportunities. My brand expanded to "turnaround CEO," "fixer," "change agent," "take-it-to-the-next-level transformer," and "global financial services expert."

Claim your identity.
Knowing your brand
simply starts with
knowing who you are.

When I reflected on my brand, I realized that many of its qualities were innate to me (high-energy, passionate), and how I applied these qualities, via my risk appetite, added to my brand as a transformational leader. (Side note: When I was a child, a family friend gave me a set of sticky notes that had an illustration of dancing hippos and read, "I thrive on stress." I loved to dance [still do] and was always doing many things: busy, busy. I put one of those sticky notes on the refrigerator, and it made me smile for years. Even as a child, I knew something about my brand.)

One team exercise I participated in many years ago has stuck with me to this day. It included sitting around a table with a facilitator, who asked us to draw a picture that represented how we saw each colleague in the room. When it was my turn to see how my colleagues had depicted me, I was treated to images of power plants, batteries, plugs, and engines or motors. The images they used to describe me captured ideas like "powers us," "energizes us," "drives us," "rallies us." I quickly learned what my brand was at that company!

As a fit CEO and leader of your life, what is your brand? What is it now, and what do you want it to be? If you are unsure, the exercise of drawing an image that represents you is a powerful tool to get at your brand. You could ask friends or colleagues to do the same. When you know what your brand is, you can leverage it to fuel your goals and direct your energy to best reach them.

Immediate and Imperfect Action

Claim your identity. Knowing your brand simply starts with knowing who you are:

- No one else is you, and that is your power.
- No one else is you, and that is what makes you valuable.
- No one else is you, and that is the best thing about you.

PEN TO PAPER

Freewrite. Put your pen to paper or your fingers on the keyboard. Let yourself get everything out of your head without judgment for a designated time—five, ten, twenty minutes. Here are some tips:

- Don't overthink it. Let yourself freewrite and see what comes up!
- If you get stuck, write twenty "I am" statements.
- Answer questions: Who am I? How do I show up in the world? What makes me valuable? What do I bring to the table—at home and at work, in relationships, and with family?

BONUS

Reach out to the five people in your life you trust the most. Ask them the following questions:

- Why do you love me?
- What stands out about me to you?
- What is one thing you see in me that I have a hard time seeing in myself?

17

Align Your Stars

I N WESTERN culture, which is so based on rational, linear thought, we often miss the richness of non-rational traditions to help understand ourselves and our primary drivers. The Chinese zodiac, the reading of stars, the enneagram, and many other systems teach us that there is an alignment of our nature that is not so much deciding our fate but certainly influencing our first reactions to information and events. I am a Dragon in the Chinese horoscope (vigorous, strong, stately, self-assured, decisive, empathetic, loyal, stately). I am an Aries in the Western zodiac (courageous, determined, confident, enthusiastic, optimistic, honest, passionate, impatient). And I am an "8" in the enneagram (Leader, Challenger, Visionary). I have to say, as you dive into these different ways of viewing your "nature," they can be a path to self-discovery and understanding how you show up, as well as how others may perceive, encounter, or react to your style.

We all need balance. So, sometimes intending to harmonize your innate tendencies (your brand or what's "written in the stars") with other aspects of yourself is wise. I work on balancing out my high energy with a more receptive mode. Sometimes this means listening—not in order to add or contribute, but listening to truly hear another person. I have long worked with the image of "two ears, one mouth"—use them in proportion! I recently saw an image of an ear inside a heart, which evoked the idea of listening with empathy, listening from your heart. I love this!

Fitness is a 360-degree experience—mind, body, heart, soul. Knowing your character helps you achieve fitness. So, although part of this book is about physical fitness, you can only be fit for life with all the aspects of your fitness developed. Rest and contemplation or meditation are critical to the soul and heart.

The more we know ourselves, the more we can step into our power and worth.

Immediate and Imperfect Action

Know your cosmic blueprint. Before you roll your eyes and turn the page, hear me out. There are many ways to learn about who we are. I consider myself a self-discovery junkie and truly believe that self-knowledge is invaluable. The more we know ourselves, the more we can step into our power and worth.

Astrology is based on astronomy, and it can be an incredibly fascinating self-discovery tool. Knowing your basic birth chart can help you understand how you show up in the world (your rising sign), what your true nature is (your sun sign), and how you process emotionally (your moon sign).

As a primer, just search "birth chart calculator" online and go to a website where you can enter in your birth time, birth date, and birth city. See what comes up. You may find yourself feeling incredibly seen and validated!

18

Slow Down to Speed Up

THROUGHOUT MY career, I have seen so many people who want to "jump in and solve." Although this spirit is wonderful in many ways, it may also significantly stall the solution to an issue or being able to tackle a challenge. Slowing down to speed up is powerful. This entails clarifying your intentions and taking time to plan the approach when there's a problem to solve.

I see this firsthand whenever I am engaged to transform a business. Prior management often knows about the problems and has tried to tackle them, but without a plan—and so, subsequently, without success. When I join a business, I start with culture. Often, the hiring

For problems large or small: step back, contemplate the challenge, let it marinate, then plan the steps to get to your goal.

entity says to me: "Rebecca, we don't have time for culture; we are in crisis." My response is always, "If we don't fix the culture, then whatever work we do in the morning will be undone in the afternoon." The saying "culture eats strategy for lunch" is alive and well. Even in crises.

Once I set up a cultural framework for a plan of attack, then I place the right people in the right roles, quickly. I hire key talent to lead the transformation. With these key hires, we can then plan for and tackle the enormous challenge ahead. I often speak with experts, interview people who have solved similar problems, and then chart the strategic and tactical course. It can be a massive undertaking—sometimes just the planning phase takes three to four months, depending on the size of the transformation. By spending a significant amount of time up front to ensure the work will not require rework or redesign, we can achieve the "big hairy audacious goals" we set for ourselves. (My professor Jim Collins from business school often cited these as the best type of goals to have.) And then the team can implement the plan with confidence and achieve successful results.

This is true in so many aspects of life. Do you just go on a trip without planning your itinerary? Do you start making a dish without a recipe? Maybe you do, at times, for adventure. But then you're probably accounting for unforeseen bumps in the road and possible kitchen disasters—the kinds of things it's best to avoid when the stakes are high.

The takeaway? For problems large or small: step back, contemplate the challenge, let it marinate, then plan the steps to get to your goal. And involve the right people to help you.

Immediate and Imperfect Action

Set yourself up for success. Preparation is key! No matter what you aim to accomplish, being mindful of the before, during, and after phases of each task is so important.

Workouts offer a perfect example of this! Without a proper warm-up or cooldown, you risk injuring yourself during or after the workout. Before any workout, be sure to prepare your body through various movements to create circulation and increase flexibility and mobility in your joints.

19

Move to Gain Momentum

MOVE THE dial. Take one step at a time. Show up. Push the ball down the field.

I can't tell you how many people tell me they get stuck. "Writer's block." My answer: Just write. Sit down and start. This is true of life. I've encountered many people who say things like, "I could never do that." Well, of course, if you don't try, you never will do that.

The path to your goal starts with one step. Take the first step and then each subsequent one. You cannot digest the entire meal in one bite! Early in my career, I was working at a large bank, leading a group in the small-business arena. One day, the CEO of the bank rang me up and said that a California senator had called and asked him to join her at an opening reception that afternoon, but he was unable to attend. He had contacted each one of his direct reports and their direct reports, but somehow no one was available, in town, or able to go. So, he asked me if I could please attend and represent the bank. I said yes and quickly met with his team to get briefed before I attended the event. I learned a lot from that day: I had no issues about being ready; I already was ready. I knew my company well, and given that small business is the heartbeat of so many communities, I was a logical next choice as a representative of the bank, but I also had a reputation as someone you could trust to show up well.

About a year later, during the last week of December, a similar thing happened. From early on in my people-management career, I had a tradition of working that week because it was such a popular vacation time for so many on my team; if I worked it, more of my direct reports and others didn't have to. It suited me well, because I could take a different week off, and everyone was immensely appreciative.

The day after Christmas, I was working in a close-to-abandoned office and again received a call from the

The path to your goal starts with one step.

bank's CEO. He needed someone to immediately begin work on a matter requiring attention (MRA) from one of our regulators. I had never addressed an MRA, but I quickly got up to speed on the issues and used the week to write a plan for addressing the MRA, thereby solving the CEO's challenge. Along with the team members present, I created a ninety-day plan to address the issue, and I executed and completed it on time, by the end of March.

I use these examples because, in both cases, I gained unique and valuable experience that I would not have if I hadn't been present and ready. Everything we do in life and all the hard work we put in—that makes us ready for each next step. Be ready. Take the next step.

Immediate and Imperfect Action

Choose low-hanging fruit. Focus on moving the needle by 1 percent every day. Feeling overwhelmed by all the things you have to do to reach a goal, see a change, or transform is totally normal. Focus on the very next step right in front of you instead of looking too far into the future. Getting ahead of yourself in your head will shut you down before you even start!

PEN TO PAPER

Reflect on these questions:

- What one thing can you focus on today?
- What one thing can you do differently today?
- What one thing can you accomplish today that moves the needle by 1 percent more than yesterday?

Clarity comes through action, not thoughts. Act on one thing, no matter how small, and watch your life transform!

PART FOUR

SELF-CARE

20

Age Fit, Fit Age

OVEMENT: ANY! Just move! Aging fit is about a commitment to care for yourself as you get older. So, *move!*

In the book *French Women Don't Get Fat,* author Mireille Guiliano offers such great advice: in order to move more, get off the bus one stop early and take the stairs, not the elevator, in buildings (not skyscrapers!) whenever possible. She also champions not eating the bread in the breadbasket before the meal arrives—wise advice!—and eating only a portion of the dessert.

The beauty of these kinds of healthy habits is that the older you get, the more fit you can be. In my fifties, I feel much healthier and fitter than I did in my twenties! (Clearly, fitness was not as much a habit then as it was a hobby!)

Every day is an
opportunity to invite
into your life the
invigorating, uplifting
fountain of youth
that is exercise.

A wonderful way to approach aging is with a "beginner's mind" and a sense of awe, not a sense of dread. Aging brings abundance: of experience, of wisdom, of perspective and insight. Enjoy those insights as you age, and stay in a learning, growing mindset that lets you intentionally take the highs and the lows with grace and optimism.

One of my favorite sayings is, "You are never too old to dream a new dream." Think: Ray Kroc reinvented McDonald's when he was fifty-two! My eighty-six-year-old mother started ukulele lessons during the COVID-19 pandemic on Zoom, and she takes walks with a light, foldable chair so she can rest at corners whenever she is too tired to walk another block. She sometimes Zooms with a friend while they walk together virtually and share their scenery. A continuous-learning-and-growth mindset fuels us as we age and keeps us young in spirit and in heart. I started RMK Group, LLC, my own company, after more than thirty years of working in corporations. Lillian started her own business, as well, after many naysayers told her not to do so.

Every day you grow a day older, and every day is an opportunity to invite the invigorating, uplifting fountain of youth that is exercise into your life. Remember, if you're in a place where a thirty-minute routine feels like too much, do ten minutes, and slowly build up to fifteen, twenty, and twenty-five minutes, until thirty minutes feels like a cinch—you will still form the habit. Even the smallest movements you didn't do yesterday but do today count. The key is to move and get your blood flowing and your heart beating. Exercise will fuel your growth mindset. (With thanks to Carol Dweck for coining that term!)

You are on a path to self-care via fitness. Make it easy and enjoyable.

Immediate and Imperfect Action

Have fun and play often. My grandfather turned eighty-nine this year and still travels around the world to do his amazing life's work. He runs an orphanage in Seoul, Korea, and I am positive that being in the constant energy of fun and play with children is what keeps him happy, young, and alive. He eagerly waits for the children to come home from school every day. They run into his office and bounce up and down with excitement for their daily dose of candy from his desk. I can vividly see the smile cross his face as they pull him into silly conversations and playful interactions. He adores it.

It's easy to lose sight of play when life gets busy and hard. When we get sucked into the seriousness of it all, it ages us quickly. It wears on the soul and depletes our vitality. Choose to bring more play into your life. Create space for fun. Your inner child will thank you for it.

Here are some suggestions on how to bring more play into your life:

- Host a game night with your family.
- In your next team huddle, ask everyone to share one thing that made them smile this week.
- Text a silly selfie to a group of friends and ask them to send one back.
- Create themed dinner nights at home, complete with soundtrack.
- Volunteer to mentor a young person.
- Join an improv comedy group.
- Take a dance class you would never otherwise sign up for.

PEN TO PAPER

Reflect on where you find playful fun in your life:

- When's the last time you had fun?
- When's the last time you let yourself go and played full-out?
- What did it do for you? What made it fun?
- How can you repeat this again this week, month, or year?

21

Drink the Life Source: H2O

ABOUT 60 percent of the human body is water. The brain and heart are composed of 73 percent water, and the lungs approximately 83 percent. The skin contains 64 percent water; the muscles and kidneys contain 79 percent, and even the bones are 31 percent water.

We are made of mostly water. So, hydrate. Drink enough water to stay fresh, alert, and healthy. Keep a glass of water by your side while you work, and carry some with you when you walk, hike, or work out. Another great time to drink water is right after you wake up, as you are often dehydrated after sleeping. This also fills you up with water before breakfast, so you might eat less. If you really want to eat less, add half a fresh-squeezed lemon to your morning glass, and you will definitely feel more satiated and eat a smaller (and hopefully healthier) breakfast.

Once, after a flight I took from San Francisco to New York had landed, I was sent to the emergency room. I had shooting pain in my eyes and couldn't figure out what was going on. The culprit: dehydration. The emergency eye doctor said my eyes were so dehydrated that I was getting those zingers of pain. When he learned I traveled every week, he said, "You must drink water during the whole flight *and* put moisturizing eye drops in every hour while you're flying, before you go to sleep, and when you wake up." I have not had eye pain since! So, for you frequent travelers: drink water, and take care of your eyes with moisturizing eye drops!

Immediate and Imperfect Action

Drink a glass of water right now. I cannot stress this enough. Whenever my clients complain about feeling sluggish or having low energy, one of the first questions I ask is, "Are you hydrated?"

Hydrate. Drink enough water to stay fresh, alert, and healthy.

Hydration is *so* basic that we overlook how important drinking water is all the time! Keep a water bottle with you when you go out, ask for water frequently while flying, and always keep a big glass of water at your desk.

BONUS

There are so many additional benefits to drinking water. It also

- increases your energy
- helps you maintain focus
- flushes out toxins
- promotes regularity
- brightens skin and improves its elasticity
- boosts immunity

22

Start New Habits for Eating Fit

FOOD IS both a fuel and a pleasure; it can be both at the same time—energizing and delicious.

So, breakfast! You can't fuel your day on empty. What does your brain need in the morning? Water, protein (for example, cottage cheese, eggs, lox), healthy fat (nut butter, avocado), and good carbohydrates filled with fiber (whole grains, fruit). You need all the food groups to power you. I often start my day with eggs, fruit, water, and tea. I also love a breakfast of whole-grain toast with peanut butter and some berries. Or yogurt and berries. The options are endless. The key is to start your day right.

Everything in moderation, including moderation!

I went off caffeinated coffee long ago, but I do get a bit of caffeine in the morning with black tea. Then, throughout the day, I drink water, decaf coffee, or green tea. Later in the day, I switch to herbal tea, so no more caffeine that might disrupt my sleep cycle.

I aim for healthy lunches and dinners, too. When I am out for lunch, I usually order a salad with protein and dressing on the side. At home, I make salads with protein (often tuna—an amazing source of protein and very low calorie). I eat fish, a few vegetables, and rice or another carbohydrate for dinner, along with a glass of wine. (I love a good glass of wine.) I find that a real meal leaves me satisfied and full, physically and mentally.

I do not deprive myself of desserts; I just take it easy on them. I eat ice cream, cookies, cakes, and so on, as a dessert or snack—but in moderation. For instance, if my family brings home a box of doughnuts, I cut one in half or thirds and have a taste rather than the whole thing. If there's chocolate cake, and if I plan to eat a whole slice, I will dial down the bread or something else in my meal so I have room for cake.

When I travel, I bring small packs of nuts, dried salmon jerky, small energy bars, and dried fruit. Many times, I have sat on a tarmac for hours while an airplane was stuck in "hold pattern" (I have done this for up to six hours!), and the airline attendants handed out only water and cookies! However, I did not have to live on cookies and air because I always pack healthy and delicious snacks.

What you put in your mouth is the fuel that feeds your brain, heart, and body.

I have heard so many approaches to dieting and fitness and read many books on the topic. My favorite is *French Women Don't Get Fat,* which I also referenced in chapter 20. Mireille Guiliano has such a pragmatic approach to eating for pleasure and health that it is one of the only books I recommend to folks, and it is a fun read.

Everything in moderation, including moderation! Don't deprive yourself. Also, don't overdo it—that is not a good feeling, either. And *always* enjoy.

Immediate and Imperfect Action

Eat to satiety. This means to eat to satisfaction. It is so common to under-eat or overeat. I have had so many clients tell me they don't know if they have had enough unless they are uncomfortably full. I have also had clients over the years who are so afraid of gaining weight that they consistently under-eat.

Both practices can lead to weight and mood fluctuations. At worst, they can lead to poor energy management and other health issues. At your next meal, nourish your body with healthy fats, proteins, and fiber-rich carbohydrates. Eat until you feel satisfied, but stop before your stomach starts hurting.

Eat slowly and mindfully, and allow your body to fill up with the nourishment you need. It takes twenty minutes for your brain to know that your belly is full. If you start to feel full, it is time to slow down and eventually stop.

23

Pay Yourself First

SHORTLY AFTER arriving home after graduate school and about to start my first job, I attended a lecture hosted by the Financial Women of San Francisco. A member was giving a session on financial planning. She said that if the audience took away only one thing from the talk, it should be this: pay yourself first.

The takeaway was so simple and so powerful. When you get your paycheck, the first person you pay is yourself: your long-term savings (home, retirement, business plan) and your short-term savings (vacation, car, home improvement, and so on). The money you retain *after* paying into your savings is what you can spend.

Paying yourself first is one of the most profound ways to take care of yourself. And the discipline of planning, budgeting, and paying yourself first is equally apropos to mental and physical fitness. Start your day by "paying yourself first"—I often do this with a five-to ten-minute meditation practice, or I take time just to stare into space, to clear my mind, and then I begin my day focused on my key goals. This mental exercise pays off in droves throughout the day, especially when everything—meetings, calls, emails, requests, emergencies, and more—starts coming at me in spades. To pay myself first physically, I prioritize my thirty minutes of exercise every day. These kinds of short breaks are like adding money to a savings account, only you're depositing mental and physical energy in the bank.

Immediate and Imperfect Action

Invest in yourself. This is the ultimate act of self-love. You declare that you are worthy. You solidify the belief that you are the most reliable investment. Pouring time, energy, and money into improving or bettering yourself can only produce great outcomes. When you pour into

The discipline of planning, budgeting, and paying yourself first is equally apropos to mental and physical fitness.

your own cup first, you increase your capacity to give back to the people and causes you care about most.

Give yourself permission to invest in personal training, therapy, a coach, or leadership training. Support, accountability, and mentorship expedite growth and results. Your future self will thank you for it. The people in your life and the world will experience the greater ripple effect, too.

PEN TO PAPER

Reflect on investing in yourself:

- What do you need help with?
- In which areas of your life would you like to see expedited growth and results?
- How might your life improve if you seek help or invest in yourself?
- What action can you take this week toward investing in yourself?

24

Get Your Sleep

S LEEP IS a window into your mental, physical, and spiritual health. Good sleep is the ultimate in self-care and the key to total health. During sleep, your body regenerates and repairs itself.

Sleep is critical for not only your body but also your mind and soul. Many factors can contribute to poor sleep. But if you're not sleeping well, consider whether your mind is processing your life unconsciously—for instance, solving a problem that you didn't solve during the day. My parents were medical doctor Jungian psychoanalysts (in other words, psychiatrists). They taught me at an early age to keep a pen and paper by my bed to write down my dreams in the morning, because, once the day progresses, we tend to

The better the quality of sleep you get, the more focused and energized you will be throughout the day!

forget our dreams. Dreams are a portal into our unconscious lives.

My mother also told me that the body doesn't forget, that it will always make up for a lack of sleep. If you don't get enough sleep at night, your body will "steal" small naps throughout the day and you'll fall asleep at your desk or in meetings or, more dangerously, behind the wheel of a car.

To share just a few secrets for getting a good night's rest: power down about an hour before you want to go to bed; don't drink caffeine starting in the late afternoon; and be physically active during the day. (Yes, getting your thirty minutes in will improve your sleep!) Before you go to bed, write down a list of things on your mind or tasks you have to accomplish the next day, so you can "let go" of your worries and to-do list before you sleep. I always tell myself, "There is nothing I can do now about tomorrow. My job now is to sleep!" You might also keep a gratitude journal next to your bed and write down what you're grateful for, which will help you start sleep off right, with positive thoughts.

Immediate and Imperfect Action

Create a morning and bedtime routine. No matter where you are in the world or what day of the week it is, consistency trains your body to know when it is time to wind down and when it's time to ramp up. The more consistent you are, the better sleep you will get. The better the quality of sleep you get, the more focused and energized you will be in the day!

Here are some things to consider for your morning and evening routines:

Morning routine:

- Choose a consistent wake-up time.
- Drink eight to twelve ounces of water upon waking.
- Get into a positive mindset with gratitude, affirmations, meditation, or journaling.
- Do a physical check-in. Stretch, or plan your workout for the day.
- Check in with your to-do list and determine top priorities for the day.

Evening routine:

- Choose a consistent bedtime.
- Shut off devices thirty to sixty minutes before bedtime.
- Do a reflection practice—meditation, gratitude, or journaling.
- Check in with yourself physically, stretching and creating a comfortable environment for sleep.

25

Keep Good Posture

I N MY travels, I have learned the hard way that sitting can cause great pain. It all started when I took on a role that had me commuting to another city weekly—a routine that lasted three years. I then moved into an international role, running a wealth-management business, and I began traveling more than two hundred thousand miles a year, to all parts of the world. I developed sciatic pain—and suffered constantly, in pain doing everything from driving to lacing up my shoes—and began serious work with a physical therapist to solve the issue. We even had calls over FaceTime when I traveled, especially to check in after a sixteen-hour flight to Singapore. But after weeks of us working together, my pain persisted, and the physical therapist was stumped.

When I returned from Singapore, the therapist asked me if she could bring a trusted colleague to our next appointment for a second opinion. That was a super instinct! The first question the other physical therapist asked me was, "Do your feet touch the floor when you are on airplanes?" I said no, and in fact, my feet rarely touch the floor when I sit on most couches, chairs, or park benches. I'm five-foot-one, and, by the way, airplane seats are built for the "average person," who is supposedly five-foot-eight—which works for no body, except a five-foot-eight body!

The question sparked a *huge* breakthrough for me. The physical therapist instructed that, whenever I sat, I was to make sure my back touched the back of the seat and my feet touched the floor. We devised an immediate plan to use my suitcase as a footrest and to carry a travel bolster (or use my rolled-up coat) for behind my back. Then we evaluated my whole "life of sitting" and added footrests under my dining room and kitchen tables, my desk, and so on. For flights, I bought a foldable footrest that I brought with me everywhere I traveled and carried to conference rooms so my feet always touched the floor. In conjunction with these changes, I dutifully practiced the exercises they gave me to strengthen key

Do you show
up in alignment
with yourself?

muscles (abs and glutes), which atrophy when we sit all day. Within weeks, my pain went away.

Before then, I never knew the power of posture; but I can tell you now, for all the sitting we do, posture is key to a pain-free life!

The metaphor for leadership, here, is so profound: alignment is a physical manifestation of how you carry yourself as a leader in the world. Do you show up in alignment with yourself? Your company? Your team? Your community? Your family? Do you give yourself the support you need? Do you stand tall?

Immediate and Imperfect Action

Open up your spine and get aligned regularly. Your posture is how you carry yourself. When you enter a room, you want to exude confidence and authority and be approachable, all at the same time.

When your spine and posture are out of alignment, you feel physical discomfort. When you experience discomfort, it affects the way you show up, your performance and focus. A little realignment and readjustment throughout your day goes a long way.

Get out of your seat, stretch often, and keep your joints and posture in check.

Get in Your Body

Practice these simple movements to improve your posture, whether you are sitting or standing:

- seated neck rolls
- seated shoulder rolls
- standing spine opener
- arms overhead chest opener
- chest opener against the wall or in a doorway

Note: Consult "Getting into Your Fitceo Body" at the back of the book for details about the best way to do these movements.

26

Rest and Recover

R EST IS different from sleep. Rest is a time to re-charge, but in smaller doses. It can be listening to music or taking a short nap. Rest can be sitting down for a cup of tea and reading or doing a puzzle. It is about consciously slowing down. I am often productive, running around, getting things done. I have learned to stop, sit, and rest. It is critical. You can't show up for yourself or for others if you are frazzled. Or exhausted. I have led teams from hundreds to thousands, and I have learned that how I look and feel—and the energy I project—are critical, as they role model the way for others.

My most profound encounter with exhaustion was as a new mother. When I was pregnant, my mother and

You can't show up for yourself, or for others, if you are frazzled.

others told me to "rest when the baby rests." I heard them, smiled, and moved on. I had no idea, really, what they meant. Until I had my first child. Early on, when he napped, I wrote thank-you letters, cleaned, organized—I kept busy. But I quickly realized what all those experienced mothers meant, because the baby would wake up at night when I was sleeping and exhausted. My son's pediatrician used to say, "Sleep deprivation is a form of torture, so make sure you rest and sleep!" Soon I began to rest when my son napped, and I felt much better.

My second most profound encounter with exhaustion was in turning around a troubled business. Solving regulatory problems, changing a culture, and meeting with a board of directors monthly is nothing short of tiring! I learned to manage my energy by choosing to walk every day, even when we worked crazy hours. I walked outside in the morning, at lunchtime, and then before dinner. This enabled me to refresh my thoughts and perspective, because we were literally working morning, noon, and night to solve urgent and important issues.

Still, I know I am not the best at rest. Sitting for a minute to let my mind and body rest—literally rest—takes a certain effort. I have learned that if I take a break to rest, pause, meditate (breathe), or stare into space, I can be fully present for my team as a leader. Being fully present and listening to the person in front of me allows me to be there for them. It is a reminder that paying myself first is the best way to help others.

Immediate and Imperfect Action

Develop a meditation practice. There are so many benefits to a regular meditation practice. Meditation creates space between the thousands of thoughts that run through the mind each day. It is incredibly healing and restful. Meditation also

- increases self-awareness
- improves mental focus
- expands compassion for others
- pulls you into the present moment
- decreases stress and negative thoughts
- reduces feelings of depression, anxiety, anger, and restlessness

To start a regular meditation practice, focus on consistency. It is far better to sit in meditation for five or ten minutes a day than to try to meditate for longer periods of time scattered throughout the week.

There are many ways to get started! Meditation can be as simple as setting a timer for five minutes and sitting still. Try this with your eyes closed, focusing on your breath. Pay attention to how your breath comes in and out through your nose as you inhale and exhale. Whenever your mind wanders (which it will), gently bring your focus back to your breath, and let yourself enjoy the stillness.

We've included resources for meditation instruction and guided meditation at the end of the book.

PART FIVE

HEART

27

Strike a Balance

WHEN I am interviewed on business panels, people often ask how I balance it all. I always answer, "There is not necessarily balance in every day, but there is balance in a whole life." I often describe periods of work as "sprints" (for example, month-end close or plan development) and other aspects of work as a "marathon" (the day-to-day activities that keep the business running). We are mostly in a marathon, but we choose where we need to sprint, like when we have a pressing client issue or a product release. Balance means connecting with your primary intention, your center, your heart, and not forgetting what brings you joy—in other words, leading with your heart.

It is a lofty goal to have balance, and I do not always achieve it. Hardly ever. However, I do try to have a "whole life," and fitness supports that.

If you lead a busy life, finding balance is all about creating a discipline that is fun and enjoyable and that provides results without stress. *No stress!* Who needs more? So, if you have a day when you can't do thirty minutes of movement, do twenty, or ten—whatever you can fit into your schedule without overdoing it. When I frequently traveled around the globe, some mornings when my alarm rang, my body was still on West Coast time, even though I was physically on the East Coast, or in Europe or Asia, and getting up thirty minutes early was just too difficult. On those mornings, I would do a quick set of sit-ups, push-ups, and stretches for ten to twelve minutes to start my day; I felt more awake just by moving my body. Then later, if I could, I would go for a quick walk. Sometimes, when I had an interview, I would ask the candidate if they were up for a stroll. Those were often my most productive interviews. Honestly, sitting across from someone with a résumé is so intimidating. This way, if the candidate was sweating, it was because they were walking, not because of the stress of the interview!

Know what feels good, and do what feels good!

Balance can also be about showing up at work, at home, and with your friends and loved ones; fully owning and accepting all aspects of yourself; and acknowledging the places where you find inner strength. Almost seventeen years ago, I participated in a two-year program on religious leadership. At the time, I was involved with a nonprofit board and also running a major business, and I was not sure that I had time for a two-year biweekly evening program, but when I spoke with former attendees, they used expressions like "life-changing" and "awesome program," so I decided to take the plunge. The program was both.

I had always thought that I kept strong divides between my secular and religious lives. I knew that topics like politics and religion were to be avoided at work. So, I was always only about work at work. However, this program showed me that we all bring our values to work. Through the readings and discussions, I learned that my ethics, responsibility, and "servant leadership" were firmly grounded in my spiritual roots, and I concluded that it was an honor and an immense responsibility to be called upon as a servant leader. I recognized that I had always been aligned with my spiritual self at work. What a pleasant surprise it was to realize that I already showed up at work in balance and authentically as my whole self.

Immediate and Imperfect Action

Know what feels good, and do what feels good! Pay attention to how you feel. This is key to maintaining balance physically, mentally, emotionally, and spiritually.

Feelings may be a physical sensation experienced in your body in response to an event. Or they may be a reaction to an emotion. Emotions are a universal, instinctual response to a positive or negative event. Feelings follow emotions and are influenced by memory, thoughts, perception, neurotransmitters, and hormones. Physical sensations and feelings in response to emotions go together.

Getting proficient at noticing these sensations and naming how you feel will set you free and give you the power to ask for what you need so you can maintain balance and harmony in your life. If you need some help in learning how to name how you feel, check out the link to the Feelings and Needs Inventory in the resources section at the end of this book.

Examples of physical sensations you may feel in response to an event:

* butterflies in your stomach when you are surprised with a new job offer
* a sinking feeling in your stomach when you realize someone has deceived you
* expansion in your chest when you are recognized and appreciated
* tightening in your chest when you get unexpected news

Examples of feelings you may experience in response to the emotions of an event:

* excited when you are surprised with a new job offer
* disappointed when you realize someone has deceived you
* powerful when you are recognized and appreciated
* frightened when you get unexpected news

To sum it up, knowing how you feel, naming how you feel, identifying your feelings, and catching them before reacting to them is a way to self-mastery:

* Feelings teach you how to tune in to your gut and intuition.

- Feelings give you information about what is working and what isn't.
- Feelings are how your body communicates with you.

PEN TO PAPER

Reflect and set intentions around how you want to feel.

When was the last time you felt happy, excited, or free?
- What happened? How did it feel in your body?

When was the last time you felt sad, angry, or trapped?
- What happened? How did it feel in your body?

How do you want to feel throughout your day?
- At home? At work? With your friends? With your family?

What can you *do* to ensure you stay connected to these feelings in every area of your life? What do you need to change, request, or adjust in order to make sure you are able to feel the way you want to feel? For example, let's say you want to feel appreciated and valued at work. Perhaps what you need in order to feel this way is support, collaboration, and guidance. Things you can do to produce this feeling and get your needs met may include:

- sending out an email request for a weekly meeting with your team
- asking for help on the next project so you aren't spread so thin
- setting boundaries around your calendar so you don't get overbooked

28

Manage Your Energy

ANAGING YOUR energy is about your vitality, your epicenter, your heart. People often tell me I have the energy of three people. I have reflected on this and thought that I was just "lucky." Now, after years of observing others and learning about energy management, I believe my energy is much more about how I manage myself—physically, mentally, spiritually, and emotionally.

All my life, I have eaten three meals a day. Who knew breakfast was so important? Most energy studies show that the "fuel" of "good" calories (in other words, nutritious foods) at breakfast helps you start your day on the right foot. I am also careful about how I eat. I used to be surprised to see colleagues eating lunch at their desks.

Growing up, I learned to eat lunch at a table and to focus on my food. I go outside and walk at lunchtime, too, to dine at a cafe or pick up a takeout lunch. If I do need to eat in my office, I eat at a table, not at my desk. People who eat at their desk or in meetings often may have no recollection that they ate. I give my body the calories it needs, and so, combined with getting enough rest and sleep, I wind up with an abundance of physical energy.

For mental energy, I do what I love. Doing work you don't like is the fastest way to drain your energy. I do not always love every task at work, but my work consists of enough things I love that it is fun and energy-producing. When I have to do things I don't love at work, I do them quickly or accompanied by music or a good cup of tea.

When I am focused at work, my energy is high. Distractions are energy-zapping. I have experimented with many ways to incorporate distractions into my job so they're not a "hassle." For instance, I changed my schedule so that all sixty- and thirty-minute meetings became fifty and twenty-five minutes. This small shift provided me with time to get a cup of tea/coffee/water, return a phone call, or prepare for the next meeting without feeling stressed, stretched, or overwhelmed. I have also scheduled half a day on Fridays for strategic work and thinking. Often, these blocks of time were taken over by urgent meetings, but usually at least once a month I got that time for longer-term thinking.

I also avoid multitasking because it's inefficient, reduces productivity, and increases stress. To show my team this, I used an exercise that I learned at a YPO (Young Presidents' Organization) event: have a partner time you as you count from 1 to 9 as fast as you can. Then ask the partner to time you as you say the alphabet from A to I as fast as you can. Finally, have your partner time you saying A1, B2, C3, and so on, as fast as you can until you reach I9. I have watched hundreds of people do this, and the results are striking. Counting or saying the alphabet takes just seconds, but combining the letters and numbers takes up to four times as long—and the stress is quadrupled as well. I saw people switch to their mother tongue and heard a "Tower of Babel" when we hit the third part of the exercise. Why? Because our brains "switch task"—they do not multitask. Multitasking reduces productivity and increases stress, zapping your mental energy. Focus is key. Stay on one task at a time, and fulfillment increases, as does productivity. This applies in business and at home!

To boost my emotional energy, I have used breaks, fun, gratitude, walks, and check-in calls to ensure I stay engaged and positive. For instance, I go out to lunch

Doing work you don't like is the fastest way to drain your energy.

with colleagues or team members, or I talk to a friend. Even a quick lunch with a friend is an oasis in a crazy, hectic day. I discovered that one- or two-minute music breaks on my phone can change my energy instantly and take me out of a stressful cycle. I also find walking to a coffee shop and buying another team member a coffee creates a break for me and good feelings for someone else. Showing appreciation is such a great way to boost energy! The busier the day, or the more stressful the situation, the more breaks you need to ensure your energy stays high. Think about Formula One race cars: they change their tires two to three times per race to optimize their performance. High-performing people, like high-performing cars, need frequent breaks to perform better!

For spiritual energy, giving back and making a difference in my community has boosted my energy. People have often said to me, "How do you have the time for all your nonprofit work?" But the time I give energizes me. I loved doing mock interviews with recent immigrants looking for work in the United States or helping organizations understand and better manage their finances. These activities are "easy" for me and so rewarding and enriching for the organizations I help. I have also lived my values at work, spending most of my career building high-performing teams—teams built on mutual trust, respect, and engagement to challenge each other to be the best we can be and achieve our goals. This requires frequent, productive communication; strategy setting; and check-ins, with many points of "breaking bread" together—all of which is fun for me.

The article "Manage Your Energy, Not Your Time" by Tony Schwartz and Catherine McCarthy offers great resources on energy management, including an energy quiz. (See the resources section of this book for more information on this article.)

Immediate and Imperfect Action

To better manage your energy, get in touch with the five layers of your body. Yoga talks about these five layers, or koshas:

- physical
- energetic
- mental/emotional
- wisdom/spiritual
- bliss/heart center

Change one aspect of the body and it changes all the other aspects of the body. If one area of the body is unhealthy or out of shape, it is most likely going to affect other areas of your body. For example, if your physical fitness is weak, it is likely to affect your confidence, which would ultimately influence your emotional resilience and mindset. This is why working on your physical fitness is so foundational and the easiest gateway to improving every other aspect of your health and life.

PEN TO PAPER

Reflect on how you think about your body:

- What is your relationship to your body?
- What layers of the body (koshas) do you feel most connected to?
- What layers of the body would you like to get more familiar with and why?

29

Be Authentic

BEING TRUE to *you* is being true to your heart. So, I tell people: be you, be more of you. You are the person who got you here; don't try to be someone else. You, as you genuinely are, are unique. I have seen a lot of people waste energy trying to be what they are not, and in the end they are miserable.

The key to being you is knowing you. Spend the time to get to know yourself.

There are many ways to discover *you*. One of the most profound exercises I did in my thirties was write my own obituary: what did I want people to say about me when I was gone? It was a real eye-opener for me about what I was doing currently and how that aligned with what I wanted to see when I looked back on my life.

I have taken multiple personality tests over the years, Myers-Briggs probably being the first (I'm an Extrovert, Intuitive, Thinking, Judging—ENTJ). I have done many others since, and each of these tests has helped me to better understand myself and leverage my strengths. Because I am an intuitive extrovert, a job without teamwork would be wrong for me, for instance. Some introverts, however, prefer jobs with more solo work—that better suits their strengths. This is extremely oversimplified, but to underscore my point: do some of these tests online. They are not expensive. They can help you become more self-aware, and that will help you stay true to you. We list some excellent personality profile tools in the resources section of this book.

As you keep being you, you will find yourself in ever-greater alignment. Doing a job you hate or being in a relationship that is wrong for you will mess with your alignment. You won't feel right, and your energy will be sapped. Staying in alignment at work, at home, and in life is essential to being fulfilled. One of my best examples of how I am true to me at work is knowing when my stress level is rising. I tend to feel it like heat rising in my chest. This early warning bell prompts me to call a break in a meeting and move out of the space of rising

No one else is you, and that is your power.

heat. I can do this in meetings, either for myself or for anyone else who I sense could use a break. I can also just leave a meeting for a bio break if needed. The bottom line: don't feel stuck if you need to take care of *you*.

For me, authenticity is a kind of integrity with myself. I was recently contacted by a board that wanted to recruit me. I let them know that unfortunately it would be a conflict with another board I was about to join. They were incredibly kind and called me three times with different board members to talk me through the ways we could ask for an exemption or special permission. I declined because I realized I would not be true to myself if I was on two different boards competing in similar spaces. I stayed true to myself, and in the process, I made three new colleagues whom I could call if, in the future, there was another opportunity.

Immediate and Imperfect Action

Practice radical honesty. What is that? Developed by Brad Blanton, radical honesty is the practice of minimizing the lies you tell—white lies, lying to yourself, and so on. It is the ability to live an authentic life and be happy by telling the truth. It is a way to create connections to and stay present in your experiences. It is a commitment to see and acknowledge things exactly as they are. Through this practice, you honor the truth behind your bodily signals and sensations.

Lying is the primary cause of suffering. Withholding, inauthenticity, phoniness, and attachment to ideals is harmful. Lying catches up to you over time and may lead to bigger consequences. Lying hurts self-esteem and confidence because you are not being genuine. Practicing honesty makes life easier over time. It sets you free. It deepens love, connection, understanding, and forgiveness.

Getting honest with yourself, first, paves the way for authenticity. When you are authentic, life feels fun, light, and easy. People trust you, want to work for you, and buy into who you are without effort on your part. No one else is you, and that is your power.

BONUS

Is there a formula for practicing radical honesty? Try this:

- Observe yourself lying. Notice all the small lies and avoidance.
- Learn how to get comfortable with discomfort. Especially with yourself.
- Honor your mind and body; when you treat them well, they will return the favor.
- Face and confront things that don't feel right, instead of ignoring or distracting.
- Be aware of sugarcoating. Does this help the other person?
- Confess when you lie or when you withhold the truth.
- Practice letting people know your intentions.

30

Make It Fun!

APPRECIATE THE many leaders who said to me, "Make sure you are having fun!" Having fun is our "why," our joy center. When I started my career, my intensity and earnestness at times made having fun an aspiration rather than an actual feeling. As I grew in my career and integrated more sides of myself into my work, it became more fun. The more I was myself, the more I enjoyed myself. Early in my career, a marketing head once said to me, "Your speeches, when they aren't prepared, they are the best. When you are just you, not 'prepared Rebecca,' you are great." I listened and thought, *Wow, I could do less and be more?* What a concept. Just being me, many times, was enough. In fact, it was more than enough. It was joyous!

What makes you happy? What brings you joy?

Life is so much easier when you can make fun of yourself a bit, laugh at situations, and let go of the seriousness of it all whenever possible. A former boss used to say, "We are not performing open-heart surgery, folks. Smile. No one is going to die if we make a mistake."

I keep a copy of *Alice in Wonderland* on my desk at all times. When things get really crazy at work, that book reminds me to ask, "Who shrank the door?" The book is also a daily reminder to maintain a state of awe, which has helped me numerous times to laugh, shake my head, get perspective, and help my team laugh, too. The key to staying open and learning continually is to stay curious. Curiosity, or awe, is a fantastic tool. Curiosity opens your mind so you can bring people along, and it also allows humor to arrive in any situation, appropriately.

So, stay in awe, or keep the child in you asking, "Who shrank the door?"

Immediate and Imperfect Action

Follow your bliss and laugh often. Our bliss center, our heart, connects us to the things that we love most. We feel a sense of purpose and can tap into creative flow easily when we are connected to our bliss.

When you follow your bliss, you:

- feel a sense of gratitude for the smallest things
- find it easy to give and accept compliments
- are generous with your love
- feel enamored by the little things
- regularly feel happy and inspired
- wind up with a smile on your face
- show others the light in your eyes

When we disconnect from our bliss center, we feel lost, stuck, and confused. This is how we get restless and lack peace, even when we "look great on paper." We often forget that following our bliss is truly the key to abundance and success.

Remember to bring fun into everything you do. The next time you feel out of alignment with your bliss, ask yourself, "When's the last time I did something fun?"

Reconnect with your bliss by:

- smiling and giving eye contact to strangers
- being silly and sharing laughter with others
- getting out in nature and breathing in the fresh air

- singing at the top of your lungs in the shower or on your way to work
- dancing in your living room for no reason

PEN TO PAPER

Reflect: What makes you happy? What brings you joy?

Moving Forward as a Fit CEO

I T HAS been such a pleasure to write this book, starting in 2012 and bringing it to completion in 2021, during a global pandemic nonetheless! Doing it, we learned that even writing a book "doesn't have to be a thing," as Lillian says. We practiced what we preached: we scheduled it, we showed up, we did the work, and we had fun! Yep, we had our Monday writing sessions every week, and we kept it light and easy.

We also enjoyed rereading and rewriting sections and then pushing ourselves to make them even simpler and easier to read and practice. There were days of writer's block when we said: just write! There were questions that we brainstormed together, and there were pivots that made the book even better. Just like life. Just like leadership. We stayed flexible in our approach but steadfast in our values. We stayed true to our intention.

We hope we've inspired you to take the same approach, and that you enjoy the journey to a FitCEO life!

Getting into Your FitCEO Body

TO CREATE a do-it-yourself, thirty-minute movement sequence that can be done almost anywhere, apply this formula:

- Design a sequence of ten exercises, choosing two exercises from each of the categories below.

- Perform each exercise for one to two minutes each.

- Repeat the entire sequence two to three times.

- Take breaks as needed.

- Remember to breathe throughout the exercises.

Key Equipment

For home or travel, we recommend purchasing these items from your favorite website or shop:

- jump rope
- short resistance band
- long resistance band, with handles
- hand weights (or use wine bottles!)
- yoga block and strap

Please choose weights that feel safe yet challenging for you to use for one to two minutes at a time for any exercises that call for hand weights. Here are some recommended guidelines:

- If you are brand-new to exercise and consider yourself an absolute beginner, please work with weights in the extra-light (one to five pounds) to light (six to eight pounds) range.

- If you consider yourself moderately fit and at an intermediate level, please work with weights in the light (six to eight pounds) to medium (ten to twenty pounds) range, adding heavier weights as needed.

- If you have been participating in an exercise regimen for many years, are extremely comfortable lifting weights, and consider yourself advanced, please work with weights in any range that suits your needs. Heavy weights range from twenty-five to thirty-five pounds, and extra-heavy weights range from forty to fifty pounds or more.

Stretch, Warm Up, Cool Down

Child's Pose
From your hands and knees, push your hips back toward your heels. Allow your forehead to rest on the floor, with your arms reached out in front of you or by your ankles.

Downward Dog
From your hands and knees, lift your tailbone up and back as you straighten your legs and come onto your toes, moving into an upside-down V. Press your heels toward the floor. Spread your fingers wide, and pull your shoulders in and down your back.

Side-to-Side Stretch

Stand or kneel. Reach your right arm overhead, leaning to the left. Feel the right side of your body stretch, and create space through your ribcage. Repeat on the left side.

Forward Fold

From standing, bend at your hips and let your upper-body weight release forward so you are hanging like a rag doll. Soften your knees as needed to sink into your hips.

Kneeling Low Lunge

From downward dog position, step one foot forward in between your hands. Drop your back knee to the floor. Stack your front knee over your ankle to create a ninety-degree angle with your front leg. Slide your back leg far enough behind you that your hips can hinge forward while still maintaining the ninety-degree angle with your front leg. Place your hands on your front knee, and square your hips to the front. Reach your arms up to go deeper into the pose. Lean back to open up your chest and hips.

Upper Body

Bicep Curls

Start with arms straight, holding hand weights in each hand. Bend at your elbows to lift the weights to your shoulders. Stabilize your elbows and shoulders as you lift. Focus on engaging the bicep muscles.

Upright Rows

Start by standing tall, holding a hand weight in each hand, with your hands in front of you, about hip-width apart. Leading with your elbows, lift the weights up toward your chin, as though you were pulling your pants up to your armpits.

Tricep Dips

With a chair or bench behind you, hold the front edge of
the chair or bench with your hands while holding yourself up. Hover your hips slightly in front of the edge of
your chair. Lower down until your elbows are at ninety
degrees. Press back up and repeat.

Seated Rows

Sitting on the floor with your legs extended, loop your
long resistance band with handles around the soles of
your feet. Sit up tall, with your spine long and shoulders back. Keep your rib cage pulled in and abdominals
engaged. Pull the resistance band in toward your body.
Keep your elbows in as you bend your arms, and squeeze
your shoulders back.

Push-Ups

From hands and knees on the floor, walk your feet
back to come into plank pose (so your body is one long,

straight line). Lower your knees to the floor if you want to make this easier. Bend your elbows as you lower your body down. Keep your elbows slightly tucked in, versus out in a *T*. Press back up and repeat.

Lower Body

Squats

Stand with your feet hip-width apart. Bend your knees to ninety degrees as you push back into your hips and press your heels into the floor. (Imagine you are sitting down on a chair behind you as you lower your hips.) Keep your knees over your ankles. Press into your heels, and squeeze your buttocks as you return to standing. Keep your abdominals engaged as you lower down and lift back up.

Alternating Lunges

Take a big step forward with one foot. Bend your knee until your front leg reaches a ninety-degree angle, keeping your knee over your ankle. Lower your back knee so it hovers just above the floor, with your back leg also bent at a ninety-degree angle. Step back and repeat on the other side.

Side-to-Side Walks

Drop into a squat position with your feet hip-width apart. Take two steps to the right, leading with your right foot. Repeat on the other side by taking two steps to the left, leading with your left foot.

Wide-Stance Squats

Stand with your feet wider than hip-width apart. Keeping your knees over your ankles, bend your knees to ninety degrees. (Imagine you are sitting down on a chair behind you as you lower your hips.) Push back into your hips and down through your heels. Keep your chest up and posture upright as you lower and stand back up.

Cardio

Jump Rope

Hold the rope with your hands at hip level. Rotate your wrists to swing the rope overhead. Jump with both feet as the rope hits the floor. Repeat until the designated time is complete. Take breaks as often as needed.

Jumping Jacks

Stand up tall, with your legs together and arms by your side. Bend your knees slightly, and jump your feet apart to slightly wider than shoulder-width. Extend and reach your arms up overhead at the same time. Jump back to the starting position. Repeat until the designated time is complete. Take breaks as needed.

Ski Jumps (Side-to-Side Jumps)

Start by standing with your feet together, and breathe in. Sit back into a squat and jump to the right, leading with your right foot, and land with both feet together Repeat, jumping to the left. Repeat this side-to-side motion, shifting your weight with each repetition, until the designated time is complete. Take breaks as needed.

Walking

When you are walking, position your feet facing forward and under your hips, about three to five inches apart. Walk through the midline of your feet, not the inside or outside. Step and land with your heel first and a slight bend in the knee. Swing the opposite arm of your stepping leg forward with each step.

Core

Back Extension

Lie on your belly, with your legs fully extended behind you and arms reaching above your head or out to the side in a scarecrow position. Draw your belly button toward your spine, and engage your abs as you lift your arms, chest, and legs off the floor. Squeeze your shoulder blades together.

Bridge Pose

Lie on your back on the floor with your hands by your sides, palms facing downward, your knees bent, and your feet flat on the floor about hip-width apart, heels close to your buttocks.

Breathe in, push your hands down, and gently press your lower back to the floor so you can slowly lift your hips up first and then peel your spine off the floor, one vertebra at a time. Reach your fingers toward your heels, and lift your chest toward your chin. Keep lifting your hips up as you breathe into your chest through your nose. Exhale slowly through your nose as you lower your hips back down to the floor.

Forearm Plank

On your elbows and knees, step your feet back so your body is one long, straight line. Lower your knees to the floor if you want to make this easier. Keep your hips lifted and level with your shoulders, and hold this pose for as long as you can.

Bicycle Crunches

Lie on your back, and pull your right knee into your chest while the left leg extends straight and hovers just above the floor. With your hands laced together behind your head for support, curl your head, neck, and shoulders off the floor. Inhale and reach your left elbow toward your right knee. Keep your elbows and chest open. Exhale as you switch sides, extending your right leg, bending your left knee in, and reaching for it with your right elbow.

Bonus Poses

Figure-Four Glute Stretch

Start by lying on your back. Bring your knees into your chest. Cross your right ankle over your left knee. Reach for the back of your left thigh with both hands, lacing your right hand between your legs. Relax your head and neck into the floor. Breathe through your nose as you hold, and then switch sides.

Happy Baby

Lie on your back, and as you exhale, bring your knees into your chest. Inhale as you take hold of the outsides of your feet with your hands. (If you have difficulty reaching your feet, you can place your hands on your ankles or hold on to a yoga strap looped over the soles of your feet.) Open your knees wider than your torso, and bring them up toward your armpits. Position your ankles over your knees so your shins are perpendicular to the floor. Flex through your heels, and gently push your feet into your hands (or the strap) as you pull your hands down to create some resistance. Breathe in and out through your nose naturally.

Supine Twists

Lie on your back on the floor with your knees bent and feet flat on the floor. Open your arms out to the side in a T. Inhale as you drop both knees over to the right side. Exhale as bring both knees back to center. Inhale as you drop both knees over to the left side. Exhale as you bring both knees back to center. Repeat five times on each side.

Knees to Chest

Lie on your back on the floor, and as you exhale, bring your knees into your chest. Press your tailbone, lower back, and spine into the floor. Feel your body releasing on the floor as you breathe in and out through your nose.

Seated Neck Rolls

Start by sitting tall in a chair. Gaze up to the ceiling, keeping your neck long. Drop your right ear down toward your right shoulder. Roll your chin to your chest. Roll your head to the left as you bring your left ear to the left shoulder. Inhale and exhale through the nose slowly and thoughtfully. Repeat five times and then switch directions.

Seated Shoulder Rolls

Start by sitting tall in a chair, with arms down by your side. Rotate your shoulders by making big circles in a forward direction ten times. Repeat the circles going backwards ten times. Breathe naturally through your nose as you focus on releasing tension in your shoulders.

Standing Spine Opener

Start by standing tall, with your arms over your head. Press your hands together as you bend and reach slightly over to the right. Breathe through your nose slowly and thoughtfully for five breath cycles. Switch and repeat on the left side.

Arms Overhead Chest Opener

Start by standing tall, and inhale as you reach your arms overhead. As you exhale, lower your elbows by your side into a scarecrow position. Squeeze your shoulders back, and open your chest as you breathe in and out through your nose. Feel the middle of your chest pressing forward as your elbows press backward.

Chest Opener against the Wall or Doorway

Stand in an open doorway. Raise both arms out to the side and bend them to ninety-degree angles, with palms facing forward. Rest your palms on the door frame. Slowly step forward with one foot. Feel the stretch in your shoulders and chest. Hold for thirty seconds as you breathe in and out of your nose comfortably. Repeat as needed.

Resources

Meditation and Yoga/Postures

For great online instruction in yoga and meditation, try these resources:

- Calm app for meditation (calm.com)

- InsightTimer app for meditation (insighttimer.com)

- Feelings and Needs Inventory Worksheet (meetlillian so.com/clients)

- Gratitude Worksheet (meetlillianso.com/clients)

- Exercise Library Videos and Workouts (youtube.com/c/LillianSo)

- *Yoga with Adriene* on YouTube, for beginner to inter-mediate yoga, with ten-to-sixty-minute sessions (youtube.com/user/yogawithadriene)

- Egoscue method videos on YouTube, for posture exercises (search "Egoscue")

Personality Tests

- Myers-Briggs (myersbriggs.org)
- StrengthsFinder 2.0 (gallup.com/cliftonstrengths/en/strengthsfinder.aspx)
- Enneagram (enneagraminstitute.com)

Books and Articles

Blanton, Brad. *Practicing Radical Honesty: How to Complete the Past, Live in the Present, and Build a Future with a Little Help from Your Friends.* Stanley, VA: Sparrowhawk Press, 2000.

Brown, Jessica. "Is Breakfast Really the Most Important Meal of the Day?" BBC Future. November 27, 2018. bbc.com/future/article/20181126-is-breakfast-good-for-your-health.

Carroll, Lewis. *The Annotated Alice: Alice's Adventures in Wonderland* and *Through the Looking Glass*. Introduction and notes by Martin Gardner, original illustrations by John Tenniel. New York: Scribner, 2000.

Collins, Jim, and Morten T. Hansen. "How to Manage Through Chaos." Great By Choice, *Fortune*. October 2011. jimcollins.com/article_topics/articles/how-to -manage-through-chaos.html#articletop.

Dweck, Carol. *Mindset: The New Psychology of Success*. New York: Ballantine Books, 2016.

Frothingham, Scott. "How Long Does It Take for a New Behavior to Become Automatic?" *Healthline*. October 24, 2019. healthline.com/health/how-long -does-it-take-to-form-a-habit.

Guiliano, Mireille. *French Women Don't Get Fat: The Secret to Eating for Pleasure*. New York: Vintage, 2007.

Lakoff, George, and Mark Johnson. *Metaphors We Live By*. Chicago: University of Chicago Press, 2003.

Lally, Phillippa, Cornelia H. M. van Jaarsveld, Henry W. W. Potts, and Jane Wardle. "How Habits Are Formed: Modelling Habit Formation in the Real World." *European Journal of Social Psychology* 40, no. 6 (October 2010): 998–1009.

Li, Charlene. *Open Leadership: How Social Technology Can Transform the Way You Lead*. San Francisco: Jossey-Bass, 2010.

Longman, Molly. "This Is How Long It Really Takes to Form a Habit (Hint: It's Not 21 Days)." Refinery29. refinery29.com/en-us/2020/01/9183127/21-day -rule-form-a-habit-in-21-days.

Pritchett, Price, and Ron Pound. *Business as Unusual: The Handbook for Leading and Managing Organizational Change*. Pritchett, Lp, 2014.

Robbins, Mike. *Be Yourself, Everyone Else is Already Taken: Transform Your Life with the Power of Authenticity*. San Francisco: Jossey-Bass, 2009.

Schwartz, Tony, and Catherine McCarthy. "Manage Your Energy, Not Your Time." *Harvard Business Review* (October 2007). hbr.org/2007/10/manage -your-energy-not-your-time.

Senn, Larry. *The Mood Elevator: Take Charge of Your Feelings, Become a Better You*. Oakland: Berrett-Koehler Publishers, 2017.

Spence, Charles. "Breakfast: The Most Important Meal of the Day?" *International Journal of Gastronomy and Food Science* 8 (July 2017): 1–6.

Thompson, Derek. "A Formula for Perfect Productivity: Work for 52 Minutes, Break for 17." Business, *The Atlantic*. September 17, 2014. theatlantic.com/business/archive/2014/09/science-tells-you-how-many-minutes-should-you-take-a-break-for-work-17/380369.

About the Authors

 **Rebecca Macieira-Kaufmann** is a seasoned CEO with broad leadership experience in sales and marketing, risk management, and international business operations. She spent more than a decade at Citigroup, serving in a range of CEO, president, and general-manager roles, and previously was with Wells Fargo for thirteen years, culminating in her role as head of the small-business segment, where she built a multibillion-dollar P&L (profit and loss) division. Rebecca is known for leading highly successful business turnarounds, scaling new businesses, and expanding operations globally, along with her strong background in governance through corporate and nonprofit board experiences. She is a frequently sought-after speaker on leadership and business transformation, culture change, and building high-performing teams.

Rebecca has received numerous awards, including being named by the *San Francisco Business Times* as one of the Bay Area's 100 Most Influential Women in

Business for twelve years. In 2018, she was honored with the Fulbright Lifetime Achievement Award, having studied at the University of Helsinki, Finland, as a postgraduate Fulbright scholar. She has a BA in semiotics from Brown University and an MBA from Stanford Graduate School of Business.

In 2020, Rebecca started RMK Group, LLC (rmk groupllc.com) to advise CEOs of start-ups in all phases of growth. She helps her clients in the same way that she achieved success in the corporate world—by devising and implementing strategies based on the philosophy of four pillars of management: operational excellence, customer centricity, employee engagement, and shareholder return.

She lives in San Francisco with her husband and children.

Lillian So is an integrator and facilitator of transformation. She has more than twenty years of industry experience in creating psychological safety, group facilitation, and compassionate communication. The founder of SOfit SF Inc. and the SO method, she is also a passionate community builder and entrepreneur.

Lillian has a BSc in kinesiology from the University of Illinois in Urbana-Champaign and is a certified personal trainer, group fitness instructor, yoga educator and therapist, non-violent communication facilitator, life coach, integrative healer, and mystic. She has received over a dozen certifications in fitness and various mind-body modalities, and she has studied Jungian psychology at the International School of Analytical Psychology Zurich. She has been featured in various publications and other media for her unique methods and transformation programs. In 2018, she received an award from the Korean American Community Foundation of San Francisco for creating a holistic program aimed at alleviating the mental health problems affecting Korean Americans in the Bay Area.

Lillian's signature fitness and yoga programs have helped people all over the world transform their relationship with their bodies through intentional movement, music, and community. Her coaching programs, which attract an international audience, have helped people transform every aspect of their lives through the five pillars of the SO method: biology, programming, inner compass, communication, and manifesting.